Praise for *UNTOLD NEW MEXICO*

"*UNTOLD NEW MEXICO* is a breath of fresh air, a literary dust devil sweeping across New Mexico's people, places, and history, kicking up all kinds of interesting dramas and fascin̶a̶t̶i̶n̶g s̶t̶o̶r̶i̶e̶s that will hold you spellbound, I guarantee."

— ...̶ *̶ngro Beanfield War*

"Tightly written, de̶e̶ ...̶ative, and a real pleasure to read. Hard to beat—a genuine w̶...̶er all the way."

—Max Evans, author, *The Rounders* and *The Hi Lo Country*

"It's no easy task to keep things fresh and still convey the depth of history and experience that is New Mexico. To truly write New Mexico you must live it. The fully initiated know that a good story can come to us from just about any corner of our little multicultural *provincia:* makes no difference if you are standing on the plaza in Santa Fe, staring at a bug-eyed alien lamppost in Roswell or watching the ball game at Isotopes Park, a good New Mexico story might just come up and kick you in the pants and you just best have pen and paper in hand when this happens, lest these savvy sparks of our humanity just flutter away. In the twenty or so stories that comprise *UNTOLD NEW MEXICO,* Jason Silverman has remained open and poised long enough to receive the story as the gift that comes from living New Mexico, and in the process he has become a swift and able storyteller. Silverman's collection is going to be required reading in my Southwest Studies classes."

—A. Gabriel Meléndez, Chair and Professor of American Studies, University of New Mexico

UNTOLD NEW MEXICO

UNTOLD NEW MEXICO
Stories from a Hidden Past

Jason Silverman

Foreword by
Governor Bill Richardson

SANTA FE

Cover image: Steve Evans
Cover design: Susan von Brachel
Book design: Vicki Ahl

Sunstone books may be purchased for educational, business, or sales promotional
use. For information please write: Special Markets Department, Sunstone Press,
P.O. Box 2321, Santa Fe, New Mexico 87504-2321.

Library of Congress Cataloging-in-Publication Data:

Silverman, Jason, 1968-
    Untold New Mexico : stories from a hidden past / Jason Silverman; foreword
by Governor Bill Richardson.
    p. cm.
    Includes bibliographical references and index.
    ISBN 0-86534-493-0 (softcover : alk. paper)
    1. New Mexico — History — Anecdotes. 2. New Mexico — Biography —
Anecdotes. I. Title.

F796.6.S55 2005
978.9'05 — dc22

                                          2005029528

WWW.SUNSTONEPRESS.COM
SUNSTONE PRESS / POST OFFICE BOX 2321 / SANTA FE, NM 87504-2321 /USA
(505) 988-4418 / ORDERS ONLY (800) 243-5644 / FAX (505) 988-1025

CONTENTS

FOREWORD / **11**
Our Past and Our Future by Governor Bill Richardson

PREFACE / **13**
Learning New Mexico

WINNING IT BACK / **17**
Taos Pueblo's Victory in Washington

PANCHO INVADES / **23**
The Day America Was Under Attack

NOT FADE AWAY / **27**
Buddy Holly's Surprising Studio

 SPOTLIGHT: / OUR FAVORITE NEW MEXICO SONGS
BY JEANIE MCLERIE AND KEN KEPPELER / **31**

STATE OF INTOXICATION / **34**
Prohibition, New Mexico Style

PRECIOUS IMAGES / **39**
New Mexico's Special Place in Photographic History

 SPOTLIGHT: / NEW MEXICO PHOTOGRAPHERS CHOOSE
THEIR FAVORITE NEW MEXICO PHOTOS / **45**

EL SENADOR / **48**
New Mexico's Forgotten Civil Rights Hero

TRUCHAS FOREVER / **53**
The Final Home of the Greatest Choreographer

THE WOLF THAT ATE ALBUQUERQUE / **58**
Hoops History at the Pit

WHAT'S IN A NAME? / **62**
Navajos and Enforced English

 SPOTLIGHT: / POEM: *AN INTRODUCTION TO SLOW BOY*
BY QUINTINA DESCHENIE / **66**

FRONTIER LAW / **68**
The Assassination of a Chief Justice

 SPOTLIGHT: UNSOLVED POLITICAL MURDERS BY STEVE TERRELL / **72**

HIPPIES AND HOPPER / **75**
The Superstar of the Taos Counterculture

 SPOTLIGHT: PETER FONDA'S LOST WESTERN / **80**

THE GHOST IN THE HALL / **84**
Cimarron's Haunted Hotel

THE BIG WEEKEND / **87**
Santa Fe Indian Market

THE RISE OF PUBLIC ART / **95**
The WPA Comes to New Mexico

 SPOTLIGHT: FIVE FAVORITE WPA WORKS BY NEW MEXICO ARTISTS
BY KATHRYN FLYNN / **99**

HAIL TO THE CHIEFS / **101**
The Rise of a Basketball Powerhouse

OUR OWN HOMER / **106**
The New World's First Epic Poem

TRAILERBLAZER / **111**
How Artist Eva Mirabal Broke the Mold

AFTER THE ERUPTION / **116**
A Geologic History of the Valles Caldera

 SPOTLIGHT: NEW MEXICO, THE VOLCANO STATE
BY DR. LARRY CRUMPLER / **119**

WHEN WE WON THE VOTE / **122**
The Suffrage Movement in New Mexico

IGOR, AT YOUR SERVICE / **126**
Stravinsky Launches the Santa Fe Opera

WILE E., INDEED / **130**
Chuck Jones in Santa Fe

 SPOTLIGHT: CHUCK'S GREATEST MOMENTS
BY LEONARD MALTIN / **134**

LOSER AND STILL CHAMPION / **136**
Las Vegas's Prizefight Debacle

 SPOTLIGHT: THE MONTEZUMA RISES AGAIN / **140**

PAVING HISTORY / **143**
The Gentrification of Canyon Road

ROSWELL'S BIG PARTY / **148**
The Fiftieth Anniversary of an Unexplained Crash

GUILTY UNTIL PROVEN INNOCENT / **153**
The Execution of Louis Young

A NEW BREED OF ROMANCE / **157**
Santa Fe's *Tao of Steve*

 SPOTLIGHT: FIVE CLASSIC NEW MEXICO MOVIES
(AND TWO GUILTY PLEASURES) BY JON BOWMAN / **161**

ACKNOWLEDGMENTS / **163**

SELECTED BIBLIOGRAPHY / **164**

SOURCE NOTES / **165**

INDEX / **179**

FOREWORD
Our Past and Our Future

By
Governor Bill Richardson

My responsibility as governor of New Mexico is to work for a better future. To do the best job I can, I believe it is important to understand our past.

History can be a great teacher and resource. That's especially true in New Mexico, a place where storytelling and tradition are deeply valued. New Mexico has a rich, complex, and truly unique history and a deep respect for those who have come before us.

You can feel it as you walk our streets, look at our art and architecture, attend community events, or converse with those who were born and raised here. New Mexico's history continues to shape our state every day and in many ways.

I'm proud to call this state, with its strong connection to the past, my home. While so many places are rushing into the future, New Mexico is taking the time to understand and celebrate its past. The elders, teachers, journalists, artists, and historians who explore and share our past are cultural treasures — gifted storytellers who use their creativity and passion to inform us about New Mexico's history and culture. They help us connect our past with our present.

Untold New Mexico is a welcome addition to the long list of excellent books about our state. This collection of essays covers many different aspects of New Mexico's history, and it reminds us that learning about our past isn't just a necessity. It can also be very entertaining. I'm grateful for the book, to its author Jason Silverman, and to the many writers and historians who remind us of what a very special place New Mexico was and continues to be.

PREFACE
Learning New Mexico

A few years ago my wife Christian, who was then working in a bookstore, struck up a conversation with an older *Nuevomexicana* customer. The woman asked how long my wife had been living in Santa Fe. "Eight years," Christian told her. "Oh," the woman responded. "Welcome."

I'm sure that woman would have the same response today. After more than a dozen years as New Mexico residents, my wife and I would probably still be newcomers in her eyes. And I understand why. New Mexicans, as much as anyone in the United States, have deep roots. Many Hispanic families can trace their personal histories back to the first waves of Spanish conquistadors some 400 years ago. And some of New Mexico's Pueblo communities have existed on their ancestral land near the Rio Grande for twice that long.

In relative terms, I'm new to this place, and the sensation of being an émigré, a stranger in a foreign land, helps me to keep my eyes and ears wide open. The more attention I pay to my adoptive state, the deeper and more genuine my curiosity seems to become, and the more respect I have for New Mexico and its history. In New Mexico, history is not an abstract list of names, dates, and places. In New Mexico, with its remarkably strong sense of continuity, history is personal. Families have lived in the same compounds on Santa Fe's Canyon Road for generations. Anniversaries and rituals seem to occur on a weekly basis. Here, the past has a daily resonance.

And New Mexico offers an entirely different window into American history and culture. Most Easterners learned that American civilization was nurtured on the Eastern Seaboard and then disseminated through the untamed West. Our schoolbooks taught us this. So did our Saturday morning cartoons, our movies, and our newspapers. American popular culture was (and remains) East Coast-centric.

Anyone who spends enough time in New Mexico will come to understand that American history and culture are far more multidimensional and complex than our schools and mass media could tell us. America didn't spring from the heads of a few great men, and it didn't radiate outward from a central point. Civilizations thrived on this land long before Europeans arrived. By A.D. 900, indigenous populations had established advanced, sophisticated communities in New Mexico. The elaborate civilizations at Chaco were in full swing by A.D. 1000, and some scientists believe the population in the Southwest was larger in 1492 than it is now. Another surprise: European settlement of the United States came from two directions, moving west from Europe and north from Mexico. European settlements were built in northern New Mexico, near San Juan Pueblo, by 1598, nearly ten years before John Smith arrived in Jamestown, Virginia.

Western expansion, with its exploratory expeditions, military incursions, intrepid homesteaders, and gold rushes, wasn't always the orderly, black-hat/white-hat endeavor we saw in the movies. The "Wild West" was chaotic and often brutal, far wilder than Hollywood allowed for, or than many viewers would have been comfortable seeing. The white guys often didn't act like heroes. In New Mexico, the collision between European explorers and indigenous cultures was at times an ugly one, and the scars still remain.

But the West, including New Mexico, seemed to breed innovation and invention and tolerance, something that New Mexico's writers have long understood. "Pretentious as it sounds, and tough as it is to prove, there *does* seem to be something about New Mexico which not only attracts creative people but stimulates their creativity," Tony Hillerman once wrote. Talented New Mexicans, driven by necessity and by a maverick spirit, have left an indelible mark on American culture and politics.

For me and others I know, coming face to face with New Mexico means shedding the simple "truths" we hold about America. Learning New Mexico means embracing complexity, nuance, and the unknowable. The poet and novelist N. Scott Momaday described New Mexico as "a place that has to be seen to be believed, and it may have to be believed in order to be seen." And D. H. Lawrence described New Mexico as "the greatest experience from the outside world that I have ever had. It certainly changed me forever. . . . [I]t was New Mexico that liberated me from the present era of civilization." New Mexico, he wrote, is a place to discover "everything we don't know and are afraid of knowing."

When I began to dig into New Mexico's historical record, I discovered thrilling, surprising and disturbing stories that brought insights into this very complicated place. New Mexico played an important role in the evolution of both rock and roll and modern dance; it was the site of the first defining moment of the Native American rights movement; it was the subject of the continent's first epic poem. But it was also the national capital of political violence and one of the last places in the country where slavery was openly practiced. New Mexico has nurtured plenty of avatars and underdogs, and launched one of our country's great, if now forgotten, civil rights leaders. It also has seen its share of intolerance, xenophobia, and outright racism.

New Mexico's history is rich, instructive, relevant, and entertaining. It's also relatively unexplored. Many of New Mexico's stories remain untold, and this collection of essays offers just a few. Spend an afternoon at the library looking at old newspapers or eavesdropping at the beauty salon or talking to a fourth-generation New Mexican and you'll find plenty more.

A few notes on process: I'm a journalist, not a historian, and I researched and wrote each of these essays as a stand-alone piece. *Untold New Mexico* is a patchwork of stories and ideas that in no way is intended to be comprehensive. The chapter order is more intuitive than logical, and I hope those who read through encounter the stories the way they might encounter history in New Mexico — a bit haphazardly, with its many stories suggesting some bigger, just-out-of-view picture. Finally, a disclaimer: I'm not by any measure an expert on New Mexico or its history. I do hope that each essay offers a prism through which to view some of the many aspects of this endlessly fascinating place.

— Jason Silverman, February 2006

WINNING IT BACK
Taos Pueblo's Victory in Washington

One of President Theodore Roosevelt's greatest legacies may have been as an environmentalist. While in office, he doubled the number of national parks and transferred vast spreads of land into the newly formed National Forest Service. But for the members of Taos Pueblo, Roosevelt's policies came at a heavy cost. In 1906, Roosevelt seized, without compensation, 300,000 acres of Pueblo-owned land as part of the new 1.5 million-acre Carson National Forest.

This vast acreage included the tiny Blue Lake. Located deep within the thickly forested Sangre de Cristo range, Blue Lake had served as a ceremonial center for generations of Taos Pueblo people. The lake flows into the Rio Pueblo de Taos, which, after dropping south and west, serves as Taos Pueblo's main source of water. Taos Pueblo grew up by the banks of the Rio Pueblo around A.D. 1300 and the headwaters, at Blue Lake, became a place of prayer.

The holiness of Blue Lake was evident to outsiders, too. Mabel Dodge Luhan, who moved to Taos in 1918, wrote:

> ...the Blue Lake is the most mysterious thing I have ever seen in nature, having an unknowable, impenetrable life of its own. Most of us are used only to the awesome holiness of churches and lofty arches, cathedrals where, with stained glass and brooding silences, priests try to emulate the religious atmosphere that is to be found in the living earth in some of her secret places.

A place like Blue Lake is well worth fighting for, and the leaders of Taos Pueblo spent the bulk of the twentieth century doing just that. The battle between Taos Pueblo and the U.S. government ultimately resonated beyond the precious patch of land and northern New Mexico. The battle for Blue Lake became a key example of the "act locally, think globally" ethos that informed later activist movements. By the time the struggle to save Blue Lake became national news in the mid-1960s, more and more Americans began wondering: Were the rights our country was founded on—liberty, equality and religious freedom—being denied to the first Americans?

A bit of history: Some believe that, before the first contact with Europeans, the Taos Pueblo area was home to 20,000 residents. But disease and violence brought by the newcomers took a huge toll. By 1906, when Roosevelt seized its land, Taos Pueblo had a population of perhaps 500. By that time, the legend of Blue Lake had already grown. In the 1890s, Spaniards and Anglos began raiding the area, some with the belief that the Taos tribe had thrown their gold and silver into the lake to safeguard them.

When the U.S. seized Blue Lake, the Taos Pueblo members were still unfamiliar with U.S. law and perhaps even the notion of "owning" land. Government officials assured the tribe that Blue Lake would be protected. But Roosevelt's attitude toward Native Americans was dismissive. "To recognize the Indian ownership of the limitless forest and prairies of this continent," he wrote, "that is, to consider the dozen squalid savages who hunted at long intervals over a territory of a thousand square miles as owning it outright, necessarily implies a similar recognition of every white hunter, squatter, horse thief, or wandering cattleman."

By the 1920s, the invasion of Blue Lake was well under way. Hikers and fishermen left their trash, and loggers began clear-cutting sensitive wooded areas. In 1928, the Forest Service built a cabin on the lake, and soon the rangers were stocking non-native fish, spraying pesticides, and cutting roads into the mountainside. Cattle owned by Anglo and Hispanic ranchers grazed the area. Perhaps most troubling, the secret religious ceremonies that had taken place at Blue Lake for centuries were endangered, as the Taos tribe had no way of keeping the area private.

"We don't have beautiful structures and we don't have gold temples in this lake," Taos leader Sefarino Martinez was quoted as saying in 1966, "but we have a sign of a living god to who we pray — the living trees, the evergreen and spruce, and the beautiful flowers and the beautiful rocks and the lake itself. We have this proof of sacred things we deeply love, deeply believe."

The seizure of Native lands by the U.S. government was part of a larger project: the forced assimilation of indigenous people into mainstream American culture. With the passage of the Religious Crimes Act in 1921, tribal religions could be practiced only with the permission of the government. R. C. Gordon-McCutchan, in his book *The Taos Indians and the Battle for Blue Lake*, described how Charles Burke, the commissioner of Indian Affairs in the 1920s, once stormed a Taos Pueblo council meeting, calling the elders "half animal" and insisting they forgo their spiritual practices. Burke then had the councillors hauled off to jail.

Generations of Native people suffered under the government's American Indian policies, which were known as "termination" — they were designed to "terminate" tribal identity and push Natives into the cities. Some practices continued for generations: children were shipped to boarding schools against the will of their parents; indigenous languages were banned; religious practices were forced underground. Often with little legal basis, and sometimes in direct violation of treaties, the U.S. government seized tribal lands.

The tide began to turn with the explosion of the civil rights movements of the 1960s. Taos Pueblo leaders had never yielded in the battle over Blue Lake. They turned down land trades and offers of monetary payments. By 1967, the Taos Pueblo's quest to regain Blue Lake was backed by powerful allies: the National Council of Churches, Secretary of the Interior Stewart Udall, and newspapers, including *The New York Times* and *The Washington Post*. New Mexico governor David Cargo also was a steadfast supporter, and Congressman James Haley of Florida drafted legislation that would return Blue Lake to Taos Pueblo ownership. Haley's bill twice passed the House of Representatives. Passage was unanimous in 1968; in 1969, only two legislators cast dissenting votes.

But senator Clinton P. Anderson of New Mexico remained a defiant foe. Arguing that the return of land to Indian ownership would set a dangerous precedent, he kept Haley's bill bottled up in committee when it reached the Senate. (Anderson may have been swayed by Robert Le Sage, a friend and campaign contributor who hoped to clear-cut the heavily forested lands surrounding the lake.)

By 1970, however, Anderson found himself opposing an unlikely Taos Pueblo supporter: President Richard Nixon. Nixon, whose college football coach and mentor was a Native American activist, quickly recognized the moral implications of the case. According to aide John Ehrlichman, Nixon also understood that backing the Taos Pueblo could have negative political impact. Still, on July 7, the eve of new congressional hearings, Nixon announced his support of the Taos Pueblo.

"He had everything to lose politically," Cargo said of Nixon. "There were no votes in it, and there was a lot of opposition in the Senate. I had a lot of disagreements with Nixon over the years, but really, his Indian policy was very good."

Cargo remembers that Senator Anderson and his supporters turned the Senate proceedings into an ugly spectacle. Flimsy evidence that the tribe had polluted the lake with cans, bottles, and cigarette wrappers was introduced, and Senator Lee Metcalf of Montana — who, Cargo said, came to the Senate floor stumbling drunk — was harsh and insulting. "Maybe passage of this bill would be an encouragement and inspiration for a whole lot of Indian religions, and medicine men would spring up all over the country," he ranted. "I would hope not."

How tense were the hearings? Here's an exchange between Taos Pueblo leader Paul Bernal and Senator Quentin Burdick of North Dakota:

> Burdick: Your basis is one of religion.
> Bernal: Yes. We base it on religious principle.
> Burdick: But suppose a portion of the land ceased to be used for religious purposes?
> Bernal: We are going to use it only for religious purposes, sir.

Burdick: Suppose it ceases to be used for religious purposes sometime?

Bernal (emphatically): It is not going to be ceased!

In addition to Nixon, the Blue Lakers had a secret weapon: Juan de Jesus Romero, the tribe's spiritual leader, or cacique. Romero, for the past sixty-four years, had done his work behind the scenes, guiding tribal leaders and praying for the return of the lake. Finally, at age ninety, he stepped into the public light. "If our land is not returned to us, if it is turned over to the government for its use," the cacique told the Associated Press, before embarking on his first plane ride, to Washington, D.C., "then it is the end of Indian life. Our people will scatter as the people of other nations have scattered. It is our religion that holds us together."

The cacique's presence in Washington had an electrifying impact on the legislators. "He held the canes of Charles V and Lincoln and Richard Nixon," White House staffer Bobbie Greene Kilberg remembered in 1993. "He didn't say a word. He just held them aloft in the Senate chambers. And there was a silence. Then everybody, all 100 Senators, turned and looked at the cacique and he just stood there and nodded and then he sat down. Then the place burst into applause."

HR 471 passed the Senate, seventy to twelve, on December 2, 1970, and returned the 48,000 acres of land surrounding Blue Lake to Taos Pueblo. Nixon signed it into law on December 15, ending a historic battle and marking a new day for Native rights.

Taos Pueblo's monumental victory galvanized the nascent environmental movement; the language used by Pueblo representatives would be familiar to contemporary environmentalists. "In all of its programs the Forest Service proclaims the supremacy of man over nature; we find this viewpoint contrary to the realities of the natural world," said Bernal, in a speech to Congress in 1969. "Our traditions and our religion require our people to adapt their lives and activities to our natural surrounding, so that men and nature mutually support the life common to both. The idea that man must 'subdue' nature and bend its process to his purposes is repugnant to our people."

Equally important, the Blue Lake hearings were a watershed in the public perception of Native peoples. For the first time, articulate, passionate Native leaders were in the national spotlight. U.S. congressmen and senators, in the hallowed chambers of Washington, D.C., acknowledged America's history of abuse of Native peoples. It was clear to anyone reading their newspapers or watching TV: the first Americans had been, for centuries, denied their rights, treated as something less than full citizens. The Taos Pueblo leaders also inspired a generation of indigenous activists, who continue to this day to work for justice.

The return of Blue Lake to Taos Pueblo didn't correct the centuries of mistreatment, but Cargo believed it signaled a new direction. "It really changed the course of history," said Cargo, who listed the return of Blue Lake as the most important moment in his long career in public office. "This was a moral renaissance. This was the first time people got up and said: We have done the Native people wrong and we need to correct it."

PANCHO INVADES
The Day America Was Under Attack

The morning of March 9, 1916, the 400 or so residents of Columbus, New Mexico, woke up to the sounds of gunfire. At first, some figured the noise was drunken mischief. "Such things as cowboys firing their pistols into the air were fairly common those days," one man recalled, in 1966. But once the townspeople began hearing faint shouts of "Viva Mexico!" they knew an invasion was on. Mexico was attacking the United States! Or maybe it was Pancho Villa, that Mexican revolutionary (or bandit?), in town with his ragtag army for a quick visit.

Villa's raid on Columbus ended nearly as abruptly as it began. By 7:15 a.m., the marauders had retreated back across the border, taking with them eighty horses, thirty mules, ammo, and weapons, including 300 Mauser guns. They left behind burning buildings, seventeen dead Americans, and about ninety of their own dead and dying comrades. Villa's invasion of Columbus, located about thirty miles south of Deming in New Mexico's southwest corner, lasted just three hours; his men had ventured all of three miles onto American soil. Still, the raid became an international incident, the first of a series of events that brought the United States and Mexico to the brink of war.

Villa's raid on Columbus (which took place less than five years after New Mexico was granted statehood) stands as a notable event in the complicated, decade-long series of battles, intrigues, and coups known as the Mexican Revolution. Beginning with the overthrow of the tyrant Porfirio Díaz in 1910, Mexico became the site of a colossal series of power struggles. Francisco Madero, who helped liberate the country from Díaz, was betrayed and executed by General Victoriano Huerta in 1913. And Huerta was defeated by a coalition led by Venustiano Carranza in 1914. After surviving a series of challenges, Carranza himself was overthrown and assassinated in 1920.

The complexity of the south-of-the-border turmoil, in combination with the growing unrest in Europe, left some Americans unsure whom to root for. The colorful, unpredictable Pancho Villa, who for a period lived in El Paso, had been for years a favorite of American newspaper writers. His raids on American property, culminating with Columbus, left a sour taste in many American mouths.

Villa was born in 1878 to a family of peasants and grew into a rebellious young man. He was imprisoned at age sixteen, some say for shooting a wealthy landowner who tried to rape his sister. Villa escaped from jail and began his legendary career as a bandit. Raiding northern Mexico's wealthy estates, and sometimes sharing the booty with the less fortunate, Villa became known as Mexico's Robin Hood.

Villa also demonstrated his cruelty and viciousness, characteristics that were useful in his rise as a Mexican military leader. After the assassination of his fellow outlaw and pal Madero in 1913, for whom he had fought against Díaz, Villa recruited a huge army, turning his untrained soldiers into a fearsome force. By 1914, Villa was Mexico's greatest field marshal, a man whom revolutionary writer John Reed compared to Napoleon. Villa's genius proved key in the overthrow of Huerta, but after the hated Huerta was deposed, Villa was again betrayed, this time by his one-time ally Carranza, who seized leadership.

For a time, Villa, the rebel from the north, and Emiliano Zapata, the rebel from the south, were able to resist Carranza's rule, even controlling Mexico City. But in 1915, Zapata's and Villa's troops were overwhelmed by Carranza's armies, and Villa badly beaten twice. Enraged, and with his army whittled down to hundreds, Villa began to blame his downfall on the United States and President Woodrow Wilson, who had once encouraged him but now supported Carranza.

According to a recently rediscovered file of Villa's papers, Villa tried to encourage Zapata to join him in invading the United States, "our eternal enemy which will always be fomenting hatred and provoking difficulties and disputes among our people." The plan, as far-fetched as it was, indicates the level of betrayal Villa felt at the United States for siding with Carranza. Still, most historians agree that the raid on Columbus was likely planned as an isolated incident, a way for Villa to furnish his troops with weapons, food, and horses.

The 1916 raid began at 4:11 a.m., the time known to the minute because one of the bullets pierced a clock. Villa's first target was a store and hotel owned by Sam Ravel, who had reportedly failed to deliver a shipment of arms that Villa had paid for the year before. The hotel was burned to the ground and the store looted. Ravel had the good fortune to miss meeting Villa that night — he was in a hospital in El Paso, undergoing minor surgery.

Members of the U.S. Army's Thirteenth Cavalry posted in Columbus were among those awakened by the gunshots. Ignoring warnings that Villa's troops were gathering on the border (who, after all, would attack a U.S. military base?), the soldiers were unprepared, their weapons locked away for the night. After breaking the locks to free the guns, the soldiers had trouble identifying the Mexican bandits in the early-morning light. The Americans' commanding officer, Colonel Herbert Slocum, reportedly stumbled to the scene after the battle had begun, drunk from "a prolonged session with Mr. John Barleycorn the evening before." Nevertheless, casualties were heavier for the Mexicans, who acted more concerned (despite some shouts of "*Muerte a los gringos!*") with grabbing booty than with killing Americans.

In the hours following the raid, Americans responded with outrage. Some wondered if Germans were involved in the plot (a book published in 1980 suggested that Villa wasn't even in Columbus, and that a German spy named Luther Wertz led the attack). Others demanded a full-scale invasion of Mexico. "Wilson Determined to Get Villa," read the headline of the March 10 edition of the *El Paso Times*, and the President agreed to support a "punitive expedition" south of the border. General John J. Pershing led 10,500 troops (including a lieutenant named George Patton) from El Paso more than 400 miles into Mexico, ostensibly to find and arrest Villa. Though the soldiers didn't find Villa, they were able to practice with some new military equipment, including airplanes, trucks, and tanks, before heading to Europe to fight in World War I. The Villa expedition was the biggest manhunt undertaken by the United States until the search for Saddam and Osama some eighty-five years later.

As documents declassified in the 1970s revealed, the punitive expedition also included secret plans for Villa's assassination. These elaborate, stranger-than-fiction plots detailed the presence of Japanese spies, double agents, invisible ink, and a so-called "three-day poison," which would kill its victim over the course of seventy-two hours. At one point, the poison was actually slipped into Villa's coffee. But Villa, who seemed to defy death, used a taster to sample his food and survived that attack (there's no word on the fate of the taster).

The American troops were removed from Mexico on February 5, 1917. Skirmishes with Carranza's troops had escalated tensions, and only desperate diplomatic efforts kept Wilson from issuing the declaration of war he had written. Pershing, in a telegraph to Washington, wrote: "Villa is everywhere, but Villa is nowhere."

But Villa's day of reckoning would come on July 20, 1923, when he was assassinated on the streets of Parral, Chihuahua, by an unknown assailant. Today, Villa is officially recognized as a revolutionary hero, with *corridos* — Mexican romantic ballads — still sung in his honor: "Hero of Liberty / Whose name is copied / Who defended Mexico / Pancho Villa, Pancho Villa! / Mountain fighter."

And tiny Columbus? The townspeople apparently are not the type to hold a grudge: they've established a Pancho Villa State Park, a Pancho Villa Motel, a Pancho Villa Museum and a Pancho Villa Cantina. Let bygones be bygones, the motto might be, at least when the tourist economy is at stake.

NOT FADE AWAY
Buddy Holly's Surprising Studio

These are the birthplaces of rock and roll: Memphis, Chicago, New Orleans, the Mississippi Delta, and Clovis. That's right—the tiny town of Clovis, New Mexico, was one of the centers of the 1950s rock explosion. It was there, in a converted grocery at 1313 Seventh Street, that Charles Hardin Holley, aka Buddy Holly, recorded all of his greatest songs.

He didn't do it solo, however. Holly combined forces with Clovis native Norman Petty, a musician and self-taught producer, and together, they created a remarkable string of hits, including "Peggy Sue," "O Boy," "Rave On," "Everyday," "Words of Love," "Maybe Baby," "Not Fade Away," and "That'll Be the Day." Without Petty and his Clovis studio, it's likely that music history would have taken a different path. For the streamlined, crystal-clear style that Holly and Petty perfected, a style that could be called the Clovis Sound, was a central influence on John Lennon, Paul McCartney and Keith Richards.

Few of Norman Petty's neighbors in Clovis would have expected, or may have even known, that this quiet man would change rock-and-roll history. But a closer look at his life's work demonstrates how motivated Petty was. As a third grader at Clovis's La Casita Elementary School, he directed the school band. He started his first group, the Torchy Swingsters, while in junior high. As a professional musician in the early 1950s, he notched several hits, including a cover of Duke Ellington's "Mood Indigo."

Though successful, Petty was frustrated by the clock-watching, profit-driven industry practices of the major studios. Meaning to record the songs of the Norman Petty Trio, he purchased his uncle's vacant store, located next door to his parents' filling station, and built a state-of-the-art studio of his own. It was a visionary move. In 1954, independent music producers were a rarity, even in big cities. And Petty was just twenty-seven.

Around the same time, about ninety miles south, in Lubbock, Texas, Buddy Holly's career was blossoming, in a small-town kind of way. Musically gifted as a child, he was performing professionally by his teens, playing his own weekly radio show by sixteen and gigging throughout Texas. In 1956, with the help of country great Marty Robbins, Holly scored his first record deal. Decca Records intended to turn the nineteen-year-old Holly into a country music star.

But all three of Holly's Nashville sessions were disasters. A Decca executive called Holly "the biggest no-talent I ever worked with," and Holly was uncomfortable with the arrangements of the songs and the demands of the cutthroat music business. He returned home after the first session, watching the charts for his single and doing occasional construction jobs.

That summer, Holly made his first trip to the Norman Petty Studio in Clovis to rehearse for his second Decca session. Bringing back tales of Norm Petty's expertise, he convinced Lubbock singer-songwriter Buddy Knox to make the drive north, too. Soon, Knox's Clovis-made "Party Doll" was climbing the charts, eventually reaching number one. In the meantime, Holly grew increasingly impatient. Decca wasn't turning him into a star. Why not follow Knox's lead and do it himself?

And so he did. Immediately after Decca dropped him in January 1957, Holly contacted Petty, and in the early evening of February 24, 1957 (the studio operated only at night, due to the noise of the filling station next door), Holly and his band began making music. By 3:00 a.m., they had recorded two songs: "I'm Looking for Someone to Love" and, in just two takes, "That'll Be the Day."

Over the next fifteen months, Holly and his band, which solidified into the Crickets, recorded sixteen more classics in Clovis. The Petty-Holly relationship, at least in the studio, proved to be remarkably productive. Holly's experience with Decca in Nashville had revealed the narrow-mindedness of major label operations. With Petty in Clovis, the increasingly confident singer was encouraged to experiment and let loose his musical genius.

According to Robert Linville, it's impossible to single out either Holly or Petty as the primary force in the creation of the Clovis Sound—the two worked as a team. A Texan who made Clovis his home, Linville sang with the Roses, Petty's backup vocal group. The Roses can be heard on "It's So Easy," among other classics.

"Buddy and Norman had so much respect for each other as individuals, and had so much in common," Linville told me. "They were both years ahead of their time. Buddy was self-made, with no formal training, and Norm couldn't even read music. And they had the same sensibilities. Norm and Buddy were both perfectionists, and so we all had to be, too. That's why you are still hearing those songs today."

The Holly-Petty sessions burned with creativity, and featured many innovations: Crickets' drummer Jerry Allison playing his knees (on "Everyday") or an empty box (on "Not Fade Away"), Petty coaxing delicate, soulful sounds out of the celesta, a kind of miniature xylophone (on "Everyday"). The Clovis Sound was a product of the collective energy as much as of any single person.

The result, a crisp, timeless, and wholly distinctive music, served as inspiration and encouragement to a generation of musicians. Among the disciples were the Beatles, who saw Buddy Holly and the Crickets on their 1958 British tour. John Lennon, Paul McCartney, and company paid homage with their arthropodal choice of name, their guitar licks, and their fashion choices (Lennon once said the Beatles' first forty songs consciously mimicked Holly, and in 1975, Paul McCartney purchased the publishing rights to all of Holly's Clovis songs). The Rolling Stones scored their first hit with a cover of "Rave On," and the songs of countless other musicians, including those of Bob Dylan and Elton John, bear the imprint in one way or another of the Clovis Sound.

Though the musical explosion that Holly and Petty created was miraculous, their relationship was not without problems. Some say that Holly regretted relinquishing a portion of the writing credit for his songs to Petty. And the increasingly popular Crickets, having allowed Petty to manage their income, grew suspicious after tasting less of the fruit than they expected. Niki Sullivan, the Crickets' original rhythm guitarist, compared Petty to Jesse James, who knocked over banks in broad daylight. Hi Pockets Duncan, Holly's first manager, told an interviewer that Petty took about 90 percent of the profits, rather than the customary 10 percent.

Hard feelings notwithstanding, many of the accusations about Petty seem ludicrous. Some claim that Petty broke up the Crickets by turning the band against Holly. In the Holly biography *Rave On*, Philip Norman goes as far as to implicate Petty in Holly's tragic death, claiming that Holly wouldn't have taken the fateful 1958 flight that claimed his life had Petty not withheld earnings from Holly. Holly's death, in a plane crash in an Iowa cornfield less than two years after his first Clovis recording, remains one of the tragic moments in rock-and-roll history, and was memorialized in Don McLean's 1971 hit "American Pie."

Those who knew Petty best wholly dispute the allegations. According to Linville, Petty was fair, consistent, and honest. In any case, he deserves his place in music history. Other producers, including Sam Phillips (whose Sun Records helped launch Elvis Presley), have been inducted into the Rock and Roll Hall of Fame. Petty, who died in 1984, has been largely forgotten. The Oscar-nominated 1978 film *The Buddy Holly Story* didn't even mention Petty or Clovis, instead showing Holly recording his songs in his own garage.

Keeping Petty out of the equation is simply unfair, according to Kenneth Broad, the co-administrator of the Petty estate. Petty, after all, used tiny Clovis as a launching pad not only for Holly but also for Roy Orbison and Waylon Jennings (both Holly protégés), along with the Raton-based group the Fireballs, whose "Sugar Shack" was the biggest hit of 1963. And the Clovis-based Roses were recently inducted into the Rockabilly Hall of Fame in Nashville. The list of important musicians Petty discovered is impressive even by Nashville or New York City standards.

"[As a producer] Mr. Petty's philosophy was that creativity didn't come by the clock," Broad said. "He wouldn't rent the studio by the hour. You paid by the song, and he'd spend all the time necessary to get it right. And though there have been nasty things written about him, I've never heard anything negative about him from anyone who knew him well. He was a gracious, generous individual and a genuine good friend."

Broad and others helped restore the Norman Petty Studio to a pristine state. "It's just like the day we buried Buddy," said Linville, a pallbearer at Holly's funeral, who sometimes takes his morning coffee there and reflects on the timeless music he helped create.

Pilgrims from around the globe who come to visit see the old Baldwin piano and Hammond organ that Petty's wife, Vi (who Holly considered an honorary member of the Crickets), used to play, along with the mixing equipment, some of which Petty built himself. "People wonder why we don't use the studio today," Broad said. "It just wouldn't be the same without Mr. Petty there to turn the knobs."

SPOTLIGHT:
OUR FAVORITE
NEW MEXICO SONGS
By Jeanie McLerie and Ken Keppeler

New Mexico's music is a real hodgepodge, coming from many sources. The Spanish colonial people brought tunes from Europe, by way of Mexico, along with mandolins and fiddles—instruments that were easy to travel with. Native American music has its roots from even further back. There's also Western-style, cowboy, norteño, and mariachi music, all of which have been assimilated into the mix.

We came to northern New Mexico from Louisiana in the early 1980s, and found some older people who knew the old dances and the songs. They would tell us that their grandkids didn't want to play the fiddle and hadn't learned the music. Most of the people who remembered the music have died, and many of the songs have been forgotten. A lot of this music is no longer a living part of the culture.

We were lucky to meet many old fiddlers in northern New Mexico, most especially Cleofes Ortiz, who became our good friend and who we played many dances and concerts with.

Here are a few of our favorite songs from New Mexico, in no special order.

"Flor de las flores (Flower of the Flowers)" (traditional) A school janitor in Wagon Mound taught it to us, and we've sung it ever since—it really is the quintessential New Mexican song.

"Estas Lindas Flores (These Beautiful Flowers)" (Antonia Apodaca, Rociada) This should be the state song instead of "Oh, New Mexico." Antonia uses the word *"gentes"* which, like "peoples" in English, is a pluralization of a word that's already plural. She wants us to know that the song is about everyone in New Mexico—the Navajos, the Spanish, the Anglos.

"The Rio Grande" (Michael Combs, Santa Fe) It's like a Woody Guthrie song, following the whole length of the Rio Grande, all the way to the Gulf of Mexico.

"Fierro" (Ana Egge, Silver City and New York City) There's been a lot of mining in New Mexico, but no songs about the miners. This is about ladies who stood up to a company that wanted to plow over their church and cemeteries. It's a protest song that says so much in just three verses.

"Cancion de Chile aka Chile Verde" (Ken Keppeler, Jeanie McLerie, Paul Rangell, and Emily Abbink) We got the idea for this song from Kenny Hall, a blind mandolin player from Fresno who was playing a song about Fresno chiles. We made it into a New Mexico song.

"Albuquerque" (Johnny Lee Wills) Johnny Lee was Bob Wills' brother, and this is a cool and funny 1940s Western Swing song. People forget that Bob

Wills worked as a barber in Roy. He got one of his songs from a guy whose hair he was cutting—he locked the door until the man taught it to him.

"Cactus Song" (Jeanie McLerie, Silver City) We wrote this one for kids—and just for fun. The kids here don't like it as much because we have cactuses everywhere, but when we go somewhere else, kids love it—in Germany and England, they keep cactuses in pots, and they are just nuts for them.

"Shi'naa'sha" (traditional Navajo song) A lot of the Native American music is alive and well today because it is used in ceremonies. The Navajo kids all know this one—"Oh, that's an old grandfather song." The women wrote it after the Long Walk in the 1860s—the forced relocation of the Navajos—to give encouragement to their men, who had been imprisoned inside Fort Sumner. It's about going home, and being on a happier trail to your home and your mesas.

"Little Joe the Wrangler" (Jack Thorpe) Thorpe was from back East, but he settled in Albuquerque and published the first book of cowboy songs in 1908 in Estancia. He wrote some of them, too, including this one about a young cowboy killed in a stampede.

"The Thing That Makes You Beautiful" (Jane Voss, Aztec) All people are beautiful in their own way. A quintessential song about people of any age or style.

"Billy the Kid" (Bob Dylan) We live in Billy the Kid country. This is the *best* of the Billy the Kid songs—and there are *many*! It was written for Sam Peckinpah's movie *Pat Garrett and Billy the Kid*.

Jeanie McLerie and Ken Keppeler, known as Bayou Seco, teach fiddling, play traditional music, write songs, and collect folklore, all from their home base of Silver City, New Mexico.

STATE OF INTOXICATION
Prohibition, New Mexico Style

New Mexico's earliest experiment in eliminating liquor began in 1889, in the town of Eddy, today known as Carlsbad. The town's founder, sole landowner and leading teetotaler, Charles Bishop Eddy, included in every lease and deed a ban on the sale of booze. It wasn't long before a few enterprising souls founded Phenix, a town just south of the Eddy city limits that consisted almost entirely of bars and bordellos. After work, Eddy residents walked or rode a mile or two to Phenix to drink, fight, gamble, rent the affections of young women, and sometimes kill one another. "Frontier sin towns were synonymous with the settling of the West," wrote Lee Myers in the *New Mexico Historical Review*. "[But] Phenix was entitled to hold her profligate head high among the worst of them."

Before embarking on its own program to banish alcohol, New Mexico could have learned a lesson or two from Eddy. In a fiercely independent, hard-drinking state, legislating against the consumption of booze would be a difficult, if not impossible, task. But that's exactly what some groups wanted to do.

In the 1880s, the New Mexico branches of the Anti-Saloon League and Woman's Christian Temperance Union (WCTU) led an organized movement against alcohol. The campaign's arguments were persuasive. Throughout the 1800s, drunkenness was a national problem. Until at least the 1810s, the average white American male drank between ten and twelve gallons of hard liquor each year. By contrast, according to a 1998 study, Americans today drink an average of two gallons of booze per year, and wine and beer account for 80 percent of that amount. In the early 1800s, heavy drinking was a staggeringly pervasive fact of life. Men might have a shot before breakfast, quaff drinks throughout the day, and start a more sustained bout after work.

The WCTU and other Prohibition supporters, who had always denounced alcohol in the name of family and religion, quickly gained ground after the beginning of World War I, when, they argued, the use of valuable grains to create liquor undermined the war effort. "If we are to win this war we can cannot do it if we stay 'pickled,'" an editorial in *The Santa Fe New Mexican* argued. "We should vote 'dry' for our country's sake."

And so they did. On November 6, 1917, New Mexico's voters passed Article XXIII by a margin of three to one, with every county but Rio Arriba and Taos voting for Prohibition. The bill's passage came thanks to a well-orchestrated push by the New Mexico WCTU, which sponsored parades as well as essay and poster contests for children. The once-powerful and vocal "wets," according to *The New Mexican*, managed only a quiet lobbying effort:

> There were rumors that the saloon interests were working hard but quietly. It was almost amusing to see well-known bartenders standing some distance from the polls, and it was generally believed that they were busy in a propaganda for the wets. One or two well-known saloon keepers also were seen riding in motors to the polls, their cars filled with voters.

On October 1, 1918, after a few days of vigorous sales at bars and liquor stores, New Mexico became the twenty-sixth dry state. It was a milestone that passed nearly unnoticed. New Mexicans were preoccupied with news of the war and with the arrival of a flu epidemic, which closed all public gathering places. In fact, the enactment of Prohibition laws was only briefly recorded in the October 2 issue of *The New Mexican*, in an irony-laced article titled "King Alcohol Gives His Last Gasp at Midnight Monday."

Of course, New Mexicans never really stopped drinking. Cheap booze, created in homemade and commercial stills and smuggled from Mexico by rumrunners, remained readily available. Many legislators were hard drinkers—a truck with twenty cases of whiskey was seized en route to the 1922 Republican state convention—and they proved reluctant to give the anti-booze laws any teeth. Policing the large, sparsely populated state was an expensive, labor-intensive chore. The federal officers who oversaw enforcement of the Eighteenth Amendment in 1920 (which turned the entire country dry) rated New Mexico as worse than average in fighting illicit liquor sales.

The New Mexican, voice of the temperance movement, kept up the pressure. A bit of hypocrisy existed here, as Oliver LaFarge pointed out in *Santa Fe: The Autobiography of a Southwestern Town*: the owner-publisher of *The New Mexican,* senator-to-be Bronson Cutting, maintained "perhaps the finest wine cellar in the Southwest." Still, a 1921 editorial railed against lax enforcement of prohibition laws:

> It is estimated that there are a dozen or more moonshine stills in operation in the immediate vicinity of Santa Fe. Everyone knows that more rotgut whiskey is being sold and drunk in Santa Fe than before the days [of Prohibition]. . . . At least two persons in Santa Fe are commonly reputed to be the leaders of the bootleg industry. Nearly any well informed citizen knows their names. . . . The thing is notorious.

Notoriety aside, some of Santa Fe's notable citizens continued to take pleasure in drink. In their biography *Will S. Shuster: A Santa Fe Legend,* Joseph Dispenza and Louise Turner recount the painter's escapades with a homemade still. For parties, Shuster, the founder of the Santa Fe Fiesta tradition of Zozobra, distilled liquor while co-conspirator Jozef Bakos brought homemade beer and wine. "Shus' specialty was a raisin-apricot (and sometimes grapefruit and potato peelings) brandy-like concoction that was always eagerly awaited by the neighbors," Dispenza and Turner wrote. Shuster's diary includes a rueful description of the death of Sam McKircher in a car accident: he was "the best bootlegger and moonshiner in town."

Historian David J. McCullough, in an article for the *New Mexico Historical Review*, described one Santa Fe speakeasy, circa 1927:

> One of the more notable establishments was housed in a three-story building. . . . The quality of the drinks and the decor of the rooms changed on each floor. The first floor was for "poorer people" who wished to quench their thirst with "white mule." . . . The second floor was for those slightly more affluent who wished to ascend to "Second Heaven" . . . . Only those with a "fat wad" could make it to the third floor where good quality booze was sold. One could drink the top-floor liquor "without a chaser."

So King Alcohol, though perhaps ailing for a time, never quite died in New Mexico. (Will Rogers put it best: "Prohibition is better than no liquor at all.") By the mid-1920s, for most Americans Prohibition was personified by Al Capone: a situation that led to terror, corruption and organized crime. Frustration with Prohibition overwhelmed voters' fear of drunkenness. Although New Mexico never hosted the murderous gun battles between police and gangsters that dominated Chicago, there were arrests: a Deming man was nabbed while smuggling booze in his laundry deliveries; a pig farmer was found hiding supplies in his sty.

Even as anti-booze sentiment faltered in New Mexico, overturning the legislation was a challenge. McCullough described attempts at reform in 1927 and 1929 as "a story of hypocrisy, chicanery, Machiavellian machinations, and high comedy." The temperance movement remained powerful, but the anti-temperance movement gained followers other than saloon owners. The prominent citizens who joined the cause provided their own powerful rhetoric. In fact, their anti-Prohibition arguments ring familiar to anyone who followed former governor Gary Johnson's battle in the late 1990s against the so-called war on drugs: the laws do more damage than the booze does; prohibition costs taxpayers enormous amounts of money; making alcohol illegal strengthens a growing criminal class.

New Mexican voters finally ratified the repeal measure in September 1933; Santa Fe residents voted 2,768 to 201 to overthrow Prohibition. Most of the state celebrated: "Elks Give Old Timers Party to Celebrate Dry Repeal," *The New Mexican* wrote. "Huge Gathering Makes Merry as State Ends Long Drouth." It followed with a list of prominent citizens who attended the Elks event. King Alcohol was alive and well in New Mexico again; he has reigned, for better or worse, ever since.

PRECIOUS IMAGES
New Mexico's Special Place in Photographic History

The photographer Ansel Adams was a well-traveled man and, as friends and acquaintances knew, an articulate letter writer. But even he struggled to find the words to describe northern New Mexico: "Lookee! Roosters! Jezuz Krize but this is a great place," Adams wrote in a letter to his friends Cedric and Rhea Wright in 1929. "Such MOUNTAINS!!!! Peaks are 13,000 feet high. . . . Pines Aspins Snow Klouds Burros Swell People. . . . You gotta see this place before you die."

Adams wasn't the first photographer to go giddy for New Mexico. The state has been an essential roosting spot for photographers for more than 150 years—very nearly the entire history of photography. The list of great artists who have made pictures here includes Edward Weston, Paul Strand, and Henri Cartier-Bresson, along with pioneers like J. K. Hillers, Timothy H. O'Sullivan, Charles Lummis, and William Henry Jackson.

"The roster of photographers who have done major work in New Mexico is a microcosm of the history of photography," wrote the late Beaumont Newhall, the author of the seminal book *The History of Photography* and a longtime New Mexico resident. Those great photographers have imprinted New Mexico on our national collective conscious.

Today, with a new century and a new vision of photography unfolding, New Mexico has emerged as one of the world's great photographic centers. In addition to the dozens of significant photographers living here, Santa Fe is home to numerous photographic institutions. The College of Santa Fe's Marion Center for Photographic Arts, a cutting-edge academic and research facility, opened in 2000 and already has been described as "the Juilliard of photography." The renowned Santa Fe Photographic Workshops, held year-round in the foothills, draw professional and amateur photographers from around the country. And Albuquerque is host to the nation's first graduate photography program, founded in 1965 at the University of New Mexico. Forty years later, this program has become a legendary training ground for adventurous photo artists. The Museum of Fine Arts, Site Santa Fe, the Center For Contemporary Arts, and the Georgia O'Keeffe Museum each exhibit photography next to painting and three-dimensional art. And Santa Fe, Albuquerque, Taos, and Silver City all have galleries dedicated to photography. There's more — the biennial Photo Arts Santa Fe celebration, the annual Review Santa Fe symposium, and a steady flow of famed visitors who bring new ideas to town. (Sebastião Salgado came in for an exhibit, and by the time he left, had begun to design a new documentary photography program for the Marion Center.)

Add to this the wondrous mountains and unforgettable landscapes — the ones that so bewitched Ansel Adams — and you can make the argument that, per capita, New Mexico has become the world's best place to make and appreciate photographs.

New Mexico's love affair with the photograph probably began around 1847. That's the year of New Mexico's earliest surviving photograph, which depicts the Taos priest, journalist, and activist Antonio José Martinez. By 1852, Santa Fe had its first studio, run by Siegmund Seligman. In the post-Civil War years, New Mexico attracted a steady stream of expeditionary photographers, usually sent by the U.S. government to document the people, buildings, and landscape of a largely uncharted territory. The best of these photographers helped elevate field photography to an art form. One newspaper described William Henry Jackson, who spent considerable time in the state between 1874 and 1881, as "the greatest scenic photographer in America."

Photography then was no point-and-click hobby; these pioneers humped a wagonload of supplies and equipment. A negative, in those days, was the same size as the finished plate, and the cameras were unwieldy. Finishing a single plate could take ten detailed steps, "hard enough to do in the studio," wrote Jackson's son, "let alone on the top of a mountain in driving gales." Some made a show of their ruggedness—Timothy O'Sullivan traveled in a Civil War ambulance—and all braved the elements (J. K. Hillers nearly died from a scorpion bite while on a shoot). The pictures, however, were worth the trouble—poignant, beautifully composed shots of a place and people that seemed a universe away from America's East Coast.

Other notables who spent time in New Mexico include Ben Wittick (who died on the job, from a snakebite, at Fort Wingate), the *Los Angeles Times* editor Charles Lummis, and Adam Clark Vroman. Edward Sheriff Curtis made several trips to New Mexico, first in 1903 and then in the 1920s. His portraits continue to shape perceptions of Native Americans, and remain among the most familiar of Western images.

By the mid-1920s, new ways of thinking about art and imagery had spread to New Mexico, thanks largely to Mabel Dodge Luhan, who presided over a growing art colony in Taos. In the 1920s and 1930s, Luhan hosted the likes of Georgia O'Keeffe, Mary Austin, D. H. Lawrence, Carl Jung, Elsie Clews Parsons, and Martha Graham. Photographers were more than welcome at her home, at least for a while. According to Van Deren Coke in *Photography in New Mexico*, Ansel Adams slept at Luhan's hacienda in 1930 until she needed his room for a new visitor. Stuck for a place to stay, he sought out Paul Strand.

By 1930, Strand already was a legendary figure, the creator, in 1916, of the first series of abstract photographs. Strand was bored with the soft-focus tendencies that defined early art photography, and shared with Adams his theories of photography, which included making crystal-clear, sharply focused images. Adams listened intently, and soon retired his soft-focus lens. He also decided, after flirting with the idea of becoming a musician, to become a professional photographer. "Taos and Santa Fe," the historian Nancy Newhall wrote, "were his Rome and his Paris." Adams created *Moonrise, Hernandez, New Mexico,* one of the most recognizable images of the century, in 1941, and continued to photograph New Mexico until 1972.

Other significant modernist photographers came to New Mexico. Edward Weston's trip was paid for with a Guggenheim Foundation Award, the first given to a photographer. Willard Van Dyke made pictures of Chimayo and Laguna Pueblo. And one of Edward Knee's photographs was chosen, above paintings, drawings, murals, and sculptures, to represent

New Mexico in a national exhibit of Works Projects Administration (WPA) art in 1937.

Documentary photography also flourished in New Mexico, especially during the Great Depression, when Dorothea Lange and John Delano were making pictures for the Farm Security Administration program. This branch of Franklin Roosevelt's WPA program was responsible for some of New Mexico's iconic images, including the famous series Russell Lee shot in Pie Town and the documents John Collier Jr. created of life in Trampas. Robert Frank and Henri Cartier-Bresson made important photos while passing through.

And there was Laura Gilpin, who Van Deren Coke described as the dean of Southwest photographers, and the great naturalist Eliot Porter. Gilpin was one of the most multitalented photographers anywhere — she even mastered aerial photography — but remains best known for the fifteen years she spent photographing the Navajo people. Porter moved to Santa Fe in 1939 and lived in New Mexico until his death in 1990; his nature photographs were displayed in two solo exhibits at the Museum of Modern Art in New York.

Santa Fe's confluence of notable photographers attracted new artists to town. David Scheinbaum came to Santa Fe with the hopes of meeting his hero, the photographer and historian Beaumont Newhall, and soon became Newhall's assistant. Scheinbaum, a native New Yorker, also was well aware of the state's enormous photographic legacy.

"Wherever you are from, these images by Timothy O'Sullivan and William Henry Jackson and J. K. Hillers and Adam Clark Vroman were the images you first studied," he said. "This area of this country is engrained in all photo students everywhere. It is a place to pilgrimage to, the place that we all had in our heads from the first day. . . . Then there is Paul Strand, Ansel Adams, Willard Van Dyke and Edward Weston. . . . All of our forefathers have walked here, and worked here. . . . It's sacred ground for photographers."

By the 1960s, photography in New Mexico had gathered enough momentum to inspire an institutional infrastructure. The University of New Mexico made the first bold strike in 1965 by founding a graduate photography program within its Department of Art. It was a visionary move that quickly turned UNM into the preeminent photography school in the country. "It has a track record not unlike the Bauhaus in students who have gone on as artists, curators, scholars, and teachers," said Steve Yates, the curator of photography at the Museum of Fine Arts in Santa Fe. "It is perhaps more influential than any other institution in the history of photography."

The list of students and instructors at the UNM program include Van Deren Coke, Beaumont Newhall, Betty Hahn, Meridel Rubinstein, Anne Noggle, Joel-Peter Witkin, Robert ParkeHarrison, and Patrick Nagatani. The adventurous spirit of the UNM program flowed north to Santa Fe. By 1969, the F-22 Gallery opened, and photographers, including Gilpin, Porter, and Todd Webb, were living in town. In the mid-1980s, Andrew Smith moved his gallery from Albuquerque to Santa Fe and Scheinbaum and Russek Photography was launched. Both are now nationally recognized photography dealers.

In 1990, Reid Callanan left the Maine Photographic Workshops to open the Santa Fe Photographic Workshops. The program quickly became a success, and has drawn professional and advanced amateur photographers from around the country. In 2002, the school hosted nearly 1,600 students for 132 weeklong workshops. The organization also runs the Santa Fe Center for the Visual Arts, which produces Review Santa Fe, an annual gathering of emerging filmmakers, curators, gallery directors, and photo editors.

Many consider Photo-Eye Books and Prints, which moved to Santa Fe from Austin in 1991, to be the finest photographic bookstore in the world, with both online and in-person sales and an influential newsletter. Most photography fans make a stop at the store and its adjacent gallery a priority when coming through Santa Fe. New Mexico's newest jewel in the photography scene, the $3 million Marion Center, includes a state-of-the-art gallery space, a library and research center (the collection of Beaumont and Nancy Newhall is housed there), and a fully equipped studio space for undergraduates.

The growth of photography in New Mexico is evident in other ways. Janet Russek, the photographer and co-owner of Scheinbaum and Russek Photography, remembers that just twenty years ago, her gallery's solo shows of Diane Arbus and Edward Weston resulted in a total of four prints sold. Photography wasn't yet considered a collectable. "In the early 1980s, photography was the bottom, bottom rung," Russek said. "There was painting, sculpture, printmaking — and then there was photography. Photography is coming to an equal place, especially in the contemporary art scene, and that's huge."

The list of notables who have lived in the state in recent years include Lee Frielander, Paul Caponigro, Joan Myers, Miguel Gandert, Meridel Rubenstein, and William Clift. The chronicler of the 1960s, Lisa Law, is based in Santa Fe, as are award-winning photojournalists Steve Northrup and Tony O'Brien. "So many great photographers have lived here and come through here," said gallery owner Andrew Smith. "Photography is still a stepchild of the arts, but it is becoming more of an integral part of it. The curators and collectors have understood the importance of photography for some time, and now the general public is beginning to understand it, too."

Photography today is in flux, as digital tools change the way pictures are made. New Mexico's strong institutional base could keep it at the forefront of the developing medium. "We've seen more change in the last ten years than we did in the past hundred," said Callanan. "The digital workflow is taking over, and the buzz word is digital — there is just no denying it. And that opens up huge opportunities and possibilities, and huge challenges."

Thirty percent of the workshops at the 2003 Santa Fe Photographic Workshops involved digital techniques. The Marion Center, too, is embracing the future, with its state-of-the-art digital lab. Scheinbaum described the process young photographers use in making pictures — shooting with an old-school 8x10 camera, developing it by hand in a tray, scanning it, printing a negative, and then making prints in the sun. "When I grew up, you worked in color or worked in black and white, you did documentary, you did landscape," he said. "The lines were very thick. But here, our students take all of the technology from all of photo history and do what they do. They do it the quickest or with the best control they know. It's beautiful to watch."

As new photographic methods emerge, New Mexico's photographers are likely to discover artful ways to use them, at least if the state's unmatched track record of invention and innovation is any measure. In fact, what's remarkable to Steve Yates is that, despite the state's long history of great photography, no "New Mexico school" has emerged. The work here remains impossible to characterize. "In New Mexico, artists go beyond classical genres and approaches," Yates said. "We are unique and rich for the spectrum of visionaries and their contributions, especially compared to such centers as New York, Europe, or Latin America. Much of the new photographic history today, across the globe, was started as ideas by artists working in New Mexico."

SPOTLIGHT:
NEW MEXICO PHOTOGRAPHERS CHOOSE THEIR FAVORITE NEW MEXICO PHOTOS

Gregg Albracht, photographer and owner, Three Ravens Fine Art
   Moonrise, Hernandez, New Mexico (Ansel Adams, 1941) *Moonrise* is an icon, without a doubt. It is one of the most recognized images of the last century, and it probably says New Mexico more than any other image, even though it was taken so long ago.

Reid Callanan, director, Santa Fe Photographic Workshops
   San Sebastian (Paul Caponigro, 1982) This image speaks to me of the stark simplicity of the New Mexican landscape, its quiet power and spirit. It is a landscape that is dwarfed and dominated by the vast sky and cloud formations. This image captures all these qualities so clearly.

Rixon Reed, owner, Photo-Eye Books and Prints

Desert Form #1, New Mexico (William Clift, 1984) You look out across the basin and you see what looks almost like the back of a reptile. I've never seen anything quite like it before—it's almost as though it's from a different planet.

Janet Russek, photographer and owner, Scheinbaum and Russek Photography

Candles and Cross (Laura Gilpin, 1960) and *Kitchen Window, Tesuque, New Mexico* (Eliot Porter, 1961) These are intimate pictures of New Mexico—they aren't the big landscapes. They give you a different sense of New Mexico, of its history, its religious aspects, the adobe, the warmth of the houses, the sun beating down upon the land. Both photos give you that feeling of New Mexico.

David Scheinbaum, director, Marion Center for Photographic Arts

Buttress, Ranchos de Taos Church, New Mexico (Paul Strand, 1931) I don't like the word "favorite," but the image that drew me here is Paul Strand's *Buttress of Ranchos de Taos*. That was the image that I stared at from my armchair, dreaming. . . . I bet I've made that image fifty times. It's hard for me to drive by without stopping by and making a picture.

Andrew Smith, owner, Andrew Smith Gallery

The Photographer's Assistant (William Henry Jackson, c. 1885) This photo describes the dawn of Western photography. . . . It embodies the spirit of adventure *and* the technical expertise of the expeditionary photographers. It's not just an adventure—you had to be a great technician, an artist, and an explorer.

Steve Yates, curator of photography, Museum of Fine Arts, Museum of New Mexico

Las Meninas (Self-Portrait) (Joel-Peter Witkin, 1987), *Ambrotype of My Great Grandfather* (Van Deren Coke, 1973) and *Daguerreotype Messages to the Past* (Betty Hahn, 1973) It would be a mistake, I believe, to suggest any photographs *of* New Mexico. This would provide a shortsighted view of the photographic arts here. Over recent decades artists have not relied on the place except as a catalyst to their works—a means to other ends. Inventing and experimenting with new ideas has become central. In this spirit, I would suggest the photos from the show "Idea Photographic". These photographers are major figures who internationally personify the inventive center of photographic arts in New Mexico.

EL SENADOR
New Mexico's Forgotten Civil Rights Hero

"We believe that all men are created equal, yet many are denied equal treatment. . . . not because of their own failures, but because of the color of their skins," said President Lyndon Baines Johnson as he signed the 1964 Civil Rights Bill, the first major equal rights legislation passed since 1875. "But it cannot continue. Our Constitution, the foundation of our Republic, forbids it. The principles of our freedom forbid it. Morality forbids it. And the law I sign tonight forbids it."

Johnson must have known that this landmark piece of legislation, which banned discrimination in hiring, voting, and public areas, ensured his place in history. Did he have any regrets at that triumphant moment? Perhaps one: his friend and colleague, the late Senator Dennis Chávez of New Mexico, wasn't there to share the victory. Having served twelve years alongside Chávez in the Senate, Johnson may have remembered "El Senador" as Capitol Hill's most active, persistent advocate for racial equality.

Though he didn't live to see it, Chávez deserved some credit for the 1964 Civil Rights Act. Chávez wasn't the only advocate of equal rights on Capitol Hill; between 1944 and 1964, 114 fair-employment bills were introduced in Congress. But Chávez was probably Congress's most tireless leader on issues of equality. He was the only legislator of color for most of the thirty-two years he spent in Congress and well understood the devastating effects of institutional racism. Having lived a rags-to-riches story, Chávez brought an underdog spirit to Washington. Forty years after passage of the Civil Rights Bill, it's clear that El Senador deserves a place alongside his more celebrated fellow-crusaders, including Cesar Chavez, Rosa Parks, and Martin Luther King Jr.

Dionisio "Dennis" Chávez was born in 1888 in Los Chaves, south of Albuquerque, into an impoverished family. Forced to quit school before he turned thirteen, Chávez became a delivery boy for Charles Conroy's Highland grocery. "In those days, you didn't wait for the customers to come to you," Chávez told *The Albuquerque Tribune* in 1959. "I had to get up at 5 a.m., feed the horse, curry him, grease the wagon, hitch up, and be at the first customer's house by five minutes after seven."

Yet there was still enough time for the library; Chávez was fascinated by U.S. history, and in particular Thomas Jefferson. And activism seemed to be in his blood—he was fired after refusing to deliver groceries to strikebreaking railroad workers. When New Mexico won statehood in 1911, the twenty-three-year-old Chávez served as interpreter on William G. McDonald's successful gubernatorial campaign. By 1917, Chávez was recognized as a gifted and dedicated part of the Democratic machine and won an opportunity to serve as a clerk under New Mexico's U.S. senator Andrieus Jones.

Chávez worked in the chambers during the day and attended classes at night, graduating from Georgetown Law School in 1920—a remarkable achievement for a man who never finished the seventh grade. He was elected to the New Mexico House of Representatives in 1922 and to the U.S. Congress in 1930. Never short on ambition, Chávez then ran unsuccessfully for the U.S. Senate seat held by Republican senator Bronson Cutting. With the election still under appeal (Chávez filed allegations of fraud), Cutting was killed in a plane crash, and Chávez was appointed to take his place. He held the seat from May 11, 1935, until his death on November 18, 1962.

From the beginning, Chávez demonstrated a talent for bringing money home. During the New Deal, as historian Roy Lujan writes in the *New Mexico Historical Review*, Chávez was "primarily responsible for ensuring that New Mexico received its share of federal monies."

But Chávez also recognized his responsibility to minorities—he was a vocal supporter of President Franklin Roosevelt's antidiscrimination policies, including the short-lived Fair Employment Practice Committee (FEPC). "When boys wearing the uniforms of the Army of the United States are denied the privilege of purchasing a soft drink in a drug store," Chávez said in a speech, "I refuse to keep calm. . . . This is the time to fight back against un-American, cowardly, despicable, racial intolerance."

Soon, equal rights organizations, along with Hispanics nationwide, were looking up to Chávez as a leader on Capitol Hill. In 1944 and 1945, with civil rights leaders emboldened by the newfound rights minority soldiers had won, Chávez sponsored bills that would make the FEPC permanent. In the process, he learned some of the tactics opponents used to quietly squash troublesome legislation. But Chávez had a few of his own tricks, and in 1946 he caught the Dixiecrats, the powerful bloc of Southern Democrats, napping.

"The Senate chamber had been as peaceful as a henhouse at laying time," *Time* magazine wrote on January 28:

> Hardly a head was turned as New Mexico's harmless-looking Democratic Senator Dennis Chávez rose and said, "I move that the Senate proceed to consideration of S. 101." Too late, his startled colleagues realized that a fox had gotten loose in their midst—S. 101 was the Fair Employment Practice bill which Southern Senators mortally hate and fear. . . .Boiling at the idea of giving a Negro a white man's wage, Southern Senators planned a filibuster which would tie up all other legislation.

The successful twenty-one-day filibuster included threats (Mississippi's James Eastland said he'd talk for "two years if necessary"), thinly veiled racist and anti-Semitic references, and accusations of the bill as central to a Communist plot (one senator called it "a communistic attempt to destroy this country"). And there were personal attacks. When a senator suggested S. 101 was designed to help a state populated with "Mexicans," Chávez responded with a history lesson, reminding his Anglo colleagues that his Spanish ancestors had arrived in the Americas long before theirs. "I am an American," Chávez answered, "and am not begging the permission of anyone to be an American, notwithstanding of my national origin."

Through it all, Chávez retained his composure, arguing with the kind of passionate reason his idol Thomas Jefferson might have admired. In fact, the transcripts of the debate in the *Congressional Record* reveal a star-making performance. Chávez even demonstrated his sense of humor. When the noted pro-segregationist senator Theodore Bilbo from Mississippi began to lecture Chávez on the "glory" of the filibuster, Chávez asked, "Did he say 'glory' or 'gory'?"

Chávez stuck with his message: that equality was a fundamental American principle. "Is it not true that the preamble to the Constitution of the United States speaks as follows: 'We, the people of the United States,'" he said in a speech before Congress. "It does not say, 'We, the Irish,' or 'We, the English,' or 'We, the Scotch,' but 'We, the people of the United States.'" Though his bill was defeated, Chávez was not—his concession was both gracious and defiant. "This is only the beginning," he told Congress. "We cannot have one country for the South and another country for the other states."

By the late 1940s, Chávez, a close friend of Harry S. Truman, had become one of the most powerful men on Capitol Hill. Chávez was the fourth-most-senior senator at the time of his death and as chairman of the Subcommittees on Defense Appropriations and Public Works oversaw more than half of Congress's funding. His legacy also includes the Elephant Butte Dam and major improvements to the Pan-American Highway, which connects North America with Central and South America.

Oddly, the public-works projects remain perhaps Chávez's best-known accomplishment in New Mexico. But, upon his death in 1962 (Chávez lived to see the sit-ins and Freedom Rides in the South, but not the March on Washington), his colleagues remembered his courage and fortitude. Chávez had survived three tough elections, Washington's institutionalized racism, and two major cancer surgeries. At Chávez's Albuquerque funeral, then-vice president Lyndon Johnson was one of an estimated 10,000 mourners who paid homage. "Chávez was a man who recognized that there must be a champion for the least among us," Johnson said.

There have been other tributes to the twentieth century's most influential American Hispanic: a 1993 postage stamp bearing his image; a statue in Congress, dedicated in 1966; and *El Senador,* a documentary completed by filmmaker Paige Martinez in 2001.

One of the film's surprises is Chávez's courageous response to

Joseph McCarthy's Communist witchhunt—Chávez made what Senator Clair Engle of California later described as "one of the greatest and most eloquent statements ever made on the floor of the U.S. Senate." Chávez's famous speech also seems a summation of a life-long battle for equality and civil rights.

"I should like to be remembered as the man who raised a voice—and I devoutly hope not a voice in the wilderness," Chávez said on May 12, 1950. "I would consider all the legislation which I have supported meaningless if I were to sit idly by, silent during . . . a period when we quietly shackled the growth of men's minds."

TRUCHAS FOREVER
The Final Home of the Greatest Choreographer

Name that icon: she was one of the great mavericks of the art world, and she escaped the pressures of New York by traveling to New Mexico. Once here, the Southwest changed the way she saw the world, and the way she approached creating new pieces.

Of course, you say — that's Georgia O'Keeffe. But the description, surprisingly, also fits the iconoclastic Martha Graham. The legendary dancer and choreographer visited New Mexico numerous times, and considered it a spiritual home. Graham used Southwestern culture as the inspiration for several of her best works, was married in Santa Fe, and insisted that her ashes be scattered in the Sangre de Cristo mountains.

Graham holds an indisputable position as American original. She single-handedly invented what today is known as modern dance, liberating concert dance from the constraints of ballet. Many often mention her in the same breath as visionaries like James Joyce, Virginia Woolf, and Pablo Picasso, each of whom radicalized an artistic medium. But Graham, one could argue, is also in part a Western artist, the Aaron Copland or John Ford of modern dance.

Born in 1894, Graham first passed through the Southwest in 1908. Her family was moving from Pittsburgh to Santa Barbara, California. The six-day train journey included an Albuquerque stopover, and when Graham left the train to stretch her legs, she told herself that she must someday return to the entrancing country she had seen through the train's windows. She also remembers sharing some fruit with a Native American girl her age: "I still cannot forget the image of her tasting what I am sure were her first grapes, very slowly and deliberately," Graham wrote eighty-three years later in her autobiography *Blood Memory*.

Graham returned to New Mexico in 1930, a year after she had formed her own New York-based company. She and composer Louis Horst spent the summer relaxing in a Santa Fe cottage and touring the region. One expedition, taken with Horst and Graham's lifelong friend Agnes de Mille, ended at Zuni Pueblo, where a rain dance was being held. In her 1956 biography, *Martha: The Life and Work of Martha Graham*, de Mille remembered the trip:

> Louis and Martha, watching the proceedings, were riveted, but we left precipitously, first because we were urged to get the hell out by the masked and dancing priests, and second because it had started, perhaps in response to the magic, to rain very hard.

Those summer months in New Mexico had a tangible and immediate influence on Graham's choreography. Absorbing Native dances and Catholic masses, Graham witnessed the power of ritual as a form of both expression and survival. The role of ritual — whether found in Catholic masses or indigenous dances or Greek mythology — became a unifying theme in Graham's work, including in the landmark piece *Primitive Mysteries.*

This three-part dance, which premiered in February 1931 in New York, was inspired, de Mille wrote, by Graham's visits to "little one-room mud churches of New Mexico. [Graham] had knelt in them beside the Indians and the Mexicans, before the *santos*, the primitive figures of Christ hanging on the cross." Some have noted that the dance itself looks something like Spanish colonial art — more angular, more raw, than European secular painting and sculpture. Graham's biographer Ernestine Stodelle described *Primitive Mysteries* as "starkly simple, blunt, unadorned" in her 1984 book *Deep Song.*

It was because of *Primitive Mysteries* — which *The New York Times* in 1931 declared to be "among the choreographic masterpieces of the modern dance movement" — that Graham became the first dancer to receive a Guggenheim Fellowship.

Graham also demonstrated her affinity for New Mexico in *El Penitente*, a 1940 three-act play that grew out of her fascination for the penitente sect of Catholicism, distinct to the Southwest. (Baryshinikov danced the lead role once and, Graham said, "took the role so completely to himself that his back was absolutely red from the rope of flagellation.")

"For Martha, the Southwest recalled childhood experiences that had secretly nourished her over the years: remembrances of the Spanish mission in Santa Barbara with its kivas, or 'skyhole,' which the Indians mystically supposed led to the center of the earth," Stodelle wrote. "The mystic in Martha found its skyhole in the Southwest."

Graham famously said that dance "is not knowledge about something, but is knowledge itself," and the seeking she did while in New Mexico was more spiritual than anthropological. Rather than collecting information to use and disseminate through her work, her visits to New Mexico seemed an ongoing mission of self-discovery. The experiences in the Southwest changed the art of Martha Graham because they changed Martha Graham herself.

The best way to understand Graham's relationship to the Southwest, at least according to former Martha Graham Company principal dancer Donlin Foreman, is to study the dances inspired by her journeys there. Take the 1946 piece *Dark Meadow*, which Foreman danced in. The work features four characters, including He Who Summons, Earth Mother, and the chorus called They Who Dance Together. Graham's character was called One Who Seeks, an apt moniker.

Stodelle writes that

> ...while *Dark Meadow* takes introspection to philosophical heights, its choreography is rooted in the visceral world of bodily sensation. Movement bursts forth as though the choreographer had suddenly touched subterranean springs of compulsive-impulsive gesture: angular, slicing motions, asymmetrical jumps, rapid shifts in rhythms, and wild careenings through space.

The sets, created by Graham collaborator Isamu Noguchi, were described by *New York Times* dance critic Don McDonagh as "baffling but beautiful, like an abstract painting that suggests figuration but stops short of delineating any details sharply." Despite its abstraction, *Dark Meadow* could have been birthed out of the New Mexican landscape.

"It's a piece that has a bleak, barren look to it," Donlin Foreman said, "but it is also fertile. Everything in the piece grows, everything flowers. It's like in the desert — it can look stark, but with a rainfall you can see flowers starting to break the surface."

Some of those same qualities characterize much of Graham's work. "Vulnerability was always very important to Martha, and the Southwest has a vulnerable landscape," said Foreman, who danced for Graham from 1977 until her death in 1991, staying with the company until 1994. "Some people might see it as impregnable, impossible, but others can see it as wide open. It bakes in the sun, it freezes at night, and beneath the surface unbelievable potential resides. She may have looked at this landscape and recognized something about the human condition. The contrasts and oppositions of the landscape of the Southwest are extreme, and contrasts and oppositions are what Martha built her work on."

Graham openly acknowledged her debt to the Southwest. "The American Indian dances remained with me always," she wrote, "just like those haunting moments before sunrise in the pueblos, or my first view of the Hopi women in their squash blossom hair arrangements that I was to use in *Appalachian Spring*. . . . My times in the pueblo . . . were always times of discovery."

The fact that Graham traveled to New Mexico at least four times offers more evidence of just how important the region was to her. On September 20, 1948, Graham and her only husband, the dancer Erick Hawkins, were married in Santa Fe:

> I had only one dress that I could possibly be seen in. It was a black taffeta skirt and coat specked with red. . . . I thought it very handsome. I wore a little veil over my face. Erick couldn't resist looking over my shoulder to see what age I would put down, but I was consistent. I took off the same fifteen years that I always had.

Graham returned to New Mexico in 1949 to heal after her marriage fell apart and visited at least once more while mourning the relationship. "She came," former Graham company dancer Jacqulyn Buglisi said, "to recover from this tremendous loss, to let her feelings out. You can tell from her history that she had a great love for the Southwest."

Graham's career was one of the most celebrated of any twentieth-century artist, with the governments of the United States, Japan, Sweden, and Jordan bestowing awards upon her. She revolutionized not only her own art form, but fashion and theater, and her disciples include Merce Cunningham and Paul Taylor and a young actress named Bette Davis, who later said she "worshipped" her former teacher.

During her more than sixty years as a choreographer, Graham created 170 dances, many of which were recorded only in Graham's mind and muscles. That makes Graham's choice of northern New Mexico as her final resting place especially poignant. Her will left explicit instructions: she was to be given a memorial service at the Santuario de Chimayo and, afterward, her ashes were to be spread in Truchas.

Graham's final requests were carried out by Ron Protas, her longtime companion and the artistic director of her company at the time of her death. Protas, who told me that "Martha always held very special memories of the Southwest," has returned to northern New Mexico at least twice since. His last visit was in March 2000, when he and Craig Strong, then the producing director of the theater group Santa Fe Stages, set off to find the place where Martha's ashes rest.

Protas didn't remember the exact spot where he scattered Graham's remains, so, Strong said, the two drove around in search of something they could never quite find. After numerous dead ends and an hour of looking, the two may have begun wondering: perhaps Martha preferred not to be found. Or maybe her ashes blended perfectly with the dark, rough soil. Maybe they were carried by the wind into the snow-capped peaks of the Sangre de Cristo Mountains.

Or perhaps Graham kept herself hidden, a reminder to Protas and Strong that the process of seeking was, in itself, enough.

THE WOLF THAT ATE ALBUQUERQUE
Hoops History at the Pit

No one ever would have accused Jim Valvano of a shortage of social skills. Personable and gregarious, he was one of college basketball's more popular coaches, beloved by his players as a terrific motivator and by sportswriters as the reliable source of a good quote. Yet, in the biggest moment of his life, and with half of the country watching, poor Jimmy V couldn't find anyone to hug. It was April 4, 1983, and Valvano and his North Carolina State Wolfpack had just won their first and only NCAA Championship. They did it in shocking fashion, beating a heavily favored team just as the final buzzer went off. Now Coach Valvano was racing around the court, tie and hair flying about, in search of someone, anyone, to celebrate with.

Most college basketball fans remember that scene: the ecstatic Valvano, with a look of disbelief on his face. And most will remember that it took place at Albuquerque's University Arena, affectionately known as the Pit. The game that launched Valvano into the national spotlight — *Sports Illustrated* that week called him "an instant legend" — did the same for the Pit, and for Albuquerque.

Built in 1966, the Pit is what, in architectural vernacular, might be called an "invisible building." From the outside, it is completely nondescript, a rectangular, largely featureless box that rises just thirty-five feet above the surrounding parking lots. It looks more like a Wal-Mart distribution center than a world-class arena. But inside, the Pit is the perfect place for rabid fans to watch a basketball game.

Joe Boehning, the Pit's architect, initially intended to build a more traditional arena — an aboveground oval. But forced to cut the construction budget in half, he found an innovative solution. He'd dig a giant hole in the ground and put the court at the bottom, thus saving a bundle on construction materials. All of Boehning's 14,831 seats had a perfect view of the court, thanks to the several dozen sight-line studies he did, and he contracted an acoustical engineering firm to ensure that the place was loud, but not dangerously so.

Fans immediately fell in love with the cramped, noisy building. Demand for tickets forced an expansion in 1975, which added another 3,177 seats. Now, with 18,008 seats available, Albuquerque began dreaming the seemingly impossible dream: hosting the NCAA Final Four, one of the sports world's most prestigious events. The Final Four was generally played in supersized stadiums like the Superdome or Georgia Dome that could seat 35,000 or more. That the NCAA chose Albuquerque and the Pit, a relatively tiny arena in a relatively small city, was a surprise to everyone.

Not that any New Mexicans complained. The Final Four weekend was front-page news all week in *The Albuquerque Journal*, which called it "the biggest party in city history." The media received gift packages that included invitations to a tour of Albuquerque homes and Nambé bowls. Albuquerque hotels overflowed with sportswriters and first-time visitors; some out-of-towners were forced to commute from Socorro, Grants, and Santa Fe. One columnist offered his advice: "There are 17,000 of you and 41 taxis. You might have to double up."

Four teams, the universities of Houston, Louisville, and Georgia, and North Carolina State, came to town that weekend. Two semifinal games were to be played on Saturday, with the winners to meet in the championship on Monday. The Houston Cougars, with their number-one rank, a twenty-five-game winning streak, a 31-2 record and two of the best players in the country — the phenom Hakeem (then Akeem) Olajuwon and Clyde Drexler, both future NBA Hall of Famers — looked invincible. They even had a nickname: Phi Slamma Jamma, inspired by their propensity for dunking the ball. None of the other quarterfinalists were even considered talented enough to compete.

When Houston beat Louisville, ranked number two, in the semifinal game on Saturday, sportswriters figured the championship game was a mere formality. Several weeks earlier, few even expected the Wolfpack to qualify for the NCAA tournament. The team had started the season 9–7, and finished tied for third in their division, at 20–10. In the postseason, they had won just one game decisively; the other seven were decided either in overtime or in the game's final few seconds. Valvano seemed to enjoy the underdog status, as it made having fun that much easier. On Thursday night, he went to the Hungry Bear, an Albuquerque nightclub, and took third in a dance competition.

On Saturday, his team beat Georgia, and on Monday night, his darkhorse Wolfpack took the court against the heavily favored Cougars, in front of a packed house and a national television audience. The game remained close until the second half, when Houston took a lead. But North Carolina State clawed back.

With forty-four seconds left, and the game tied, State grabbed a rebound. Dereck Whittenberg, the team's star guard, fumbled the ball and, panicking, threw up a desperation shot. There were three seconds left. Whittenberg's shot missed the basket by several feet, but standing there to catch it was Lorenzo Charles, a forward who had scored only one field goal in the game's first thirty-nine minutes and fifty-nine seconds. His second, a dunk as the buzzer went off, gave State and Valvano a 54–52 victory. Twenty years later, it is still remembered as one of the greatest games ever.

And it was the biggest night in history for the Pit, which became known, almost overnight, as a sacred site, a place of pilgrimage for basketball junkies from around the country. In 1999, *Sports Illustrated* named the Pit the thirteenth greatest sports venue in the world, one of only two basketball arenas on the list (neither Madison Square Garden nor Boston Garden made the cut). "The site of many mind-blowing college basketball games. . . . " the article read. "The noise created by fans, which has been measured at 125 decibels — the pain threshold for the human ear is 130 — is a palpable force."

The Pit's great show at the 1983 Final Four also seemed to help Albuquerque become more than a punch line. "Under all that howling dust and tumbling tumbleweed beats a hospitality of pure gold," wrote Curry

Kirkpatrick for *Sports Illustrated*. "Or at least of silver and turquoise."

And the one who fell most deeply in love with the Land of Enchantment's biggest city? That would be Jimmy Valvano. The beloved coach, who died of a rare bone cancer at forty-seven, vowed to never forget New Mexico and the Pit. "My wife is pregnant—she doesn't know it yet," Valvano said at the postgame conference. "And we're going to name our son Al B. Querque."

WHAT'S IN A NAME?
Navajos and Enforced English

His family called him Hastiin Yazhi Bida' Vicenti, or Nephew of Little Man Vicenti. Some of his Navajo friends called him Hastiin Akalii, which roughly translates to Cowboy Man. The Anglo ranch owners dubbed him Cowboy — for his skill in breaking their horses, and because they couldn't pronounce his Navajo names. In the 1930s, Cowboy became his official name, as recorded in the files of the U.S. government.

This tale, colorful as it is, is hardly unique. For a period of time, the American government renamed nearly everyone on the Navajo Nation, the 25,000-square-mile region that spans northwest New Mexico, northeast Arizona, and southern Utah. Be it through work, school, the Bureau of Indian Affairs, or U.S. census workers, Navajo names were systematically changed to names that American government agents could remember (Cowboy's wife, Asdzaa Li Tsooi, and her sister were *both* renamed Mary). And it wasn't just people who were renamed. Many Navajo place names were replaced by English ones. Cowboy's village T'iis Tsoozi, Thin Trees, today is known as Crownpoint. Even the word "Navajo" is foreign, from the Pueblo Indian language Tewa, in which *nava* means "cultivated field," and *hu*, "mouth of a canyon." But the Navajos call themselves Diné, or the People.

As in every culture, the way the Diné describe themselves, including their land, their culture, and their family members, is central to their identity. Sigmund Freud once wrote, "a human being's name is a principal component in his person, perhaps a piece of his soul." That's why the story of Cowboy Vicenti is significant. If a man has many names, who is he? If he has two birthplaces, where does he really come from?

Certainly, the renaming of all things Diné served as a kind of erasure. Replacing a Diné name with an English one was a central element of the federally mandated program to "kill the Indian . . . save the man," as Richard Pratt, who helped design the government's Indian boarding school system, infamously recommended in 1892. Initially, the Diné might not have taken the renaming too seriously. Traditionally a Diné child is given one permanent name, to be used in ceremonies, plus a series of nicknames. So flexibility is intrinsic to the naming process.

"Many Navajo people freely changed their Anglo names as they saw fit, unlike most Anglos, who carry their surnames along for generations," explained Tina Deschenie, former director of Indian Education for the Central Consolidated Schools in Shiprock (and Cowboy Vicenti's granddaughter). Deschenie herself was born with two names: Quintina Cowboy on her birth certificate and Quintina Vicenti on her census record.

But the United States' attempts to rename the Diné people were part of a bigger program: a deliberate agenda of assimilation. It began with the first U.S.-Navajo treaty, signed in 1846, and continued in 1864 with the Long Walk, the Kit Carson-led forced relocation that left thousands of Navajos dead and removed from their traditional ways. Even into the 1970s, English-only practices forced many Navajos to abandon their cultural practices.

"There was for years a concerted effort on the part of the government to try and separate the people from their language and names," Deschenie said. "When I was in boarding school in the late 1960s, we were forbidden to talk Navajo and use Navajo names. . . . They wanted to disconnect the people from their tribal identity and Americanize them."

The efforts to force the mainstream American way of life on Native people, which affected tribes nationwide, were generally clumsy and poorly implemented. Sometimes, in the Indian boarding schools, which employed strict, often corporal discipline in training Native children, the methods could only be described as brutal. The idea of stripping Native peoples of their names was too much even for Thomas Morgan, the staunchly assimilationist Commissioner of Indian Affairs from 1889 though

1893, who criticized its renaming process. "[There seems] no good reason for continuing a custom which has prevailed to a considerable extent of substituting English for Indian names," he wrote in 1890. "Doubtless, in many cases, the Indian name is difficult to pronounce and to remember; but in many other cases the Indian word is as short and euphonious as the English word that is substituted."

Morgan's plea was often ignored, in part due to the troubles the American agents had with the often-oral Native languages. Dr. W. N. Hailmann, the general superintendent of Indian Schools in 1890, told this story in a letter condemning the "careless trifling with the nomenclature of a great race":

> An Indian policeman rode up to the government school and delivered a little boy to the superintendent. "What's his name?" inquired the superintendent. "Des-to-dah," replied the Indian in Federal blue, as he rode away. "Destodah," mused the superintendent. "Queer name, ain't it? Max will fit him very nicely for a first name." So the little fellow was duly christened "Max Destodah." It turned out, however, that *des-to-dah* was the Indian word for "don't know." The policeman had simply said he didn't know what the boy's name was.

But was that boy always to be Max Don't Know, or was he also able to hang on to the name his family gave him? In the case of the Diné, some have managed to maintain their Native names, both the ceremonial and the casual, along with their English ones. Dr. Fred Begay, a physicist at Los Alamos National Laboratory, claims to have no trouble negotiating the differences between his government job and his Navajo home.

"Many of us have two names, our Navajo names and the names that the U.S. government gave us to try and 'civilize' us," said Begay, whose Diné name is Tse'dla'a'l Biye', which means Lichen on the Rock. "The same thing for places. We still have the Navajo names. So we haven't lost anything. Most of my elders don't even speak English. They don't care about their English names, and when I go home, they don't care about my English name."

But others see the forced renaming as a greater threat. Losing one's name might mean losing a connection to one's ancestors. As a result of assimilation efforts, many of today's young people have only English names and English-speaking parents. And because of the subsequent changes of place names, most members of the younger generations don't recognize the connection between their land and their culture.

"Ch'in li meant Mouth of the River, but it got changed to Chinle, and as Chinle is no longer a description of a place," Deschenie said, citing an example. "Most students I talk to have no idea what Chinle is, and so that connection to the land has been lost. It's the same way with our clans, which are descriptions of land formations, descriptions of the earth. Today, when the students speak the names of their clans they don't know the land formations they are referring to."

North American geography depends heavily on indigenous words; more than half of U.S. state names are derived from Native languages, along with a large percentage of lakes, rivers, and everything else found on a map. Or course, translating from one language to another often led to strange results. The Nez Perce tribe was apparently named that by European settlers who were impressed by the pierced noses of the existing residents.

Still, the loss of language and of names has become a crisis for indigenous people around the world. Of the 300 languages spoken in North America 500 years ago, less than 150 still exist, and that number could drop to fifty within two generations. But many members of the Navajo Nation hold out hope for restoring their language. The Navajo Community College, for example, changed its name to Diné College, and Washington Pass was recently renamed Narbona Pass, in honor of a Diné peacemaker killed by Colonel Washington's troops in 1849. Many Diné mothers choose traditional names for their children, often in combination with American ones. Deschenie's third child was given a Navajo middle name: Dezbah, or Girl Going to War.

A movement to record and teach the Diné language is well under way, and as many as 80,000 to 150,000 Diné, between 25 and 50 percent of the estimated population of more than 300,000, speak their native language. Still, the efforts to preserve the language remain imperative in the face of today's less direct, but possibly stronger, assimilationist forces: TV, movies, and the Internet. Scan the rolls of students in the Shiprock school district and you'll find names like Michael Jordan Begay and Jagger Mick Nez.

Is there a way to reconcile the American with the Diné? Can the Diné identity survive in the face of the all-powerful, 24-7 influences of American popular culture? Genevieve Jackson, the executive director of Diné Education for the Navajo Nation, remains hopeful, listing programs such as college scholarships for students who study the language, as well as classes in history and language at every grade level. When she visits Head Start programs throughout Navajoland, she is thrilled to see three- and four-year-olds singing Diné songs and telling stories in their language. It is, she said, "a rebirth, a resurgence, a renaissance."

SPOTLIGHT:
POEM: AN INTRODUCTION TO SLOW BOY
By Quintina Deschenie

I remember the first time I needed the help of an elder
And I had to go alone, without my mother.
"Where you from?" he asked.
"To Diahia Dee', from Black Water," I said,
meaning Whiskey Creek.
"From whose place?" he asked.
"My grandfather was called 'To' Hayi i niai yee',
'The One Who Dug Wells,'" I replied.
"Uuuuuuh," he said. "The Hopi man. Kiis'aani yee.

You're from the other side of the mountain, Bini'dee'."
And then he smiled and shook my hand.
And I was so happy to be the granddaughter
Of Howella Polaaca.

Quintina Deschenie, Diñe/Hopi, lives in Farmington, New Mexico and is a poet and writer for national and local publications.

FRONTIER LAW
The Assassination of a Chief Justice

"Take it back," said William Logan Rynerson, pointing a gun at John Potts Slough. The two were standing in the lobby of the Exchange Hotel, on Santa Fe's plaza, on a cold December day in 1867.

"I don't propose to take anything back," said Slough. "Shoot and be damned." And so Rynerson pulled the trigger, sending a fatal bullet through Slough's side. John Slough, a military leader who had survived several brutal Civil War battles, died in a most unheroic way, murdered by a man he hardly knew. He didn't even have time to draw his Derringer.

That a man was killed in a public place, on a Sunday afternoon, was not in itself remarkable; in its territorial days, New Mexico was considered one of the most violent places in America. Slough, however, was chief justice of the New Mexico Supreme Court; his killer was a member of the territory's House of Representatives. This was more than murder—it was assassination.

Slough's death was a key moment in what historian Gary L. Roberts, in his book *Death Comes for the Chief Justice*, called "a period of officially condoned and/or excused violence" in New Mexico. It is likely, as suggested by historian Richard Maxwell Brown, that the murder helped affirm New Mexico's position as "apparently the only place where assassination became an integral part of the political system."

Before his sudden, violent death, Slough had become something of a legend. He was appointed chief justice in 1866 by President Andrew Johnson, whom Slough had served as a bodyguard. And Slough was also close with the White House's previous occupant, Abraham Lincoln, serving as a pallbearer at his funeral. Johnson probably figured Slough was a good man to send to New Mexico; in 1862, Slough had led the First Colorado Volunteer Regiment in action at Glorieta, located outside of Santa Fe, in a Civil War battle that many believe won the West for the Union.

An Ohio native, Slough came to New Mexico with a reputation as a hotheaded but honorable man. Several times, his temper landed him in trouble. He twice struck fellow Ohio legislators (he was expelled from Ohio's House of Representatives) and also was charged with assault by a Virginia citizen who claimed he had used abusive language. Once he settled in Santa Fe, Slough became known largely as an independent-minded judge whose determination to fight corruption often overwhelmed New Mexican protocol.

In fact, Slough seemed to have a blind spot for all things political. He ruled his court with too heavy a hand. Historian Calvin Horn described him as having "an exceptional command of abusive language, which he used masterfully and willingly against any opponent." Slough would suspend without pay any jurors he suspected to have been bribed, and once imprisoned a man who yelled out the name of a political figure during a court session. Citizens dreaded appearing before this newcomer, who favored American law above New Mexico's traditional methods of governance. Slough greeted any resistance with fits of rage. He once impulsively decided to resign (a decision he rescinded the next day), and told Governor Robert Byington Mitchell to "take the Chief Justiceship and . . . stick it up his Royal Bengal a**."

Slough's anger frequently got the best of him (his obscene rants were legendary), yet he left an important legacy. While in New Mexico, the judge tried to dismantle the tainted, highly political system of patronage that defined the New Mexican courts. "Slough's crusade for judicial reform did not derive from a mean-spirited contempt for New Mexican custom and usage but from a determination to put the judicial house in order," Roberts wrote.

Slough's most controversial moment came in February 1867, when he ruled in favor of a "peon" named Thomas Heredia. In post-Civil War

New Mexico, peonage — in which captured Native Americans were forced to work, without pay, for Hispanic and Anglo bosses — remained a socially sanctioned and legally acceptable form of slavery. Slough, who had risked his life during the Civil War to help the United States end slavery, was not about to let it exist under his nose, even if fighting peonage meant alienating some of New Mexico's most powerful men.

Inevitably, the powers that were began plotting Slough's removal. In the autumn of 1867, a resolution condemning Slough, secretly penned by General Herman H. Heath, secretary of the New Mexico territory, was introduced by Rynerson, a newly elected Republican from Dona Ana County. The resolution's eleven charges included "tyrannical, overbearing" behavior on the bench, unfair and intimidating treatment of jurors, drunkenness, assault and battery, and foul language.

The resolution passed committee on December 14, 1867. That night, Slough sought out Rynerson, describing him loudly, but behind his back, as "a son of a bitch and a thief . . . a coward, but the damned scoundrel has not the courage to take it up." Slough then left, after admitting to a friend that he had gone out of his way to pick a fight. The next morning, Rynerson found Slough at the Exchange Hotel, and demanded that the judge retract his insults. One bullet and less than twenty-four hours later, Slough died from his wounds.

The newspaper coverage of the murder and the subsequent trial demonstrates just how bitterly partisan the population remained in the years following the Civil War. *The New Mexican* claimed that Slough got exactly what he deserved:

> The grossest and most obscene scurrility was heaped, by his ever voluble tongue, upon many of the first citizens of the territory . . . Men were forced to go armed day and night, ready to defend themselves, lest they should be murderously attacked by him.

But *The Santa Fe Weekly Gazette* eulogized Slough as a great man:

> The deceased was a gentleman of high mental cultivation, unsurpassed social qualities, connected with an elevated sense of

honor, which made him quick to resent wrong offered to himself, and equally prompt to do justice to others.

Rynerson was tried by a judge who, according to the *Gazette*, was "determined that Justice should be deprived of her dues, and that no punishment should be inflicted for the perpetration of the most horrid crime that was ever committed in this community." Once acquitted, Rynerson became a powerful force in New Mexico politics, an alleged member of the Santa Fe Ring, a cabal of businessmen said to dictate policy from behind closed doors.

Rynerson's acquittal may have served to reinforce New Mexico's lawless reputation, and numerous other politically motivated murders took place in the subsequent decades. "New Mexico was sparsely populated in the 1870s, but it is doubtful whether there has ever been another place in the United States where so many men were indicted for murder and so few convicted," wrote W. Eugene Hollon in his book *Frontier Violence: Another Look.* "Little wonder New Mexico won the reputation as the worst-governed place in the United States, a reputation that continued far into the twentieth century."

No monument to Slough stands in Santa Fe. At the La Fonda Hotel (formerly the Exchange Hotel), the site of the murder, by the lobby newsstand, is unmarked. ("We don't commemorate assassinations," La Fonda owner Sam Ballen said.) But Slough's legacy can be found about a hundred yards away. The obelisk located in the center of the Santa Fe plaza was dedicated to soldiers killed in the Civil War. This memorial was one of Slough's pet projects. Though Slough's name isn't listed, he also was a casualty of a country divided.

SPOTLIGHT:
UNSOLVED POLITICAL MURDERS
by Steve Terrell

1. Albert J. Fountain. A Civil War veteran, former leader of the Texas State House, newspaper editor, and U.S. district attorney, Fountain ran against Albert Fall for a seat in New Mexico's Territorial Legislature in 1888. The two stood on opposite sides of the most divisive issue of the era: Fountain strongly advocated statehood, while the Democrats, led by Fall, opposed it. Fountain won the election and was elected Speaker of the House, but then was defeated by Fall two years later. Fountain returned to his legal practice, where he aggressively pursued cattle rustlers, including several of Fall's political allies. In 1895, thanks to his investigations, a Lincoln County grand jury indicted several of them.

During the grand jury proceedings, someone reportedly handed Fountain a note: "If you drop this we will be your friends. If you go on with it you will never reach home alive."

He didn't. On January 30, 1895, Fountain and his eight-year-old son set out on a buckboard to Mesilla from Lincoln. Three men on horseback followed him. A stagecoach driver advised Fountain to turn back, but he declined. Later, Pat Garrett—yes, the man who shot Billy the Kid—found two blood-soaked patches of ground where he speculated the Fountains were killed.

Two of Fall's cronies were tried and acquitted for the murders. Their lawyer? Albert Fall himself. Did Fall have Fountain killed? We'll never know. We do know that Fall went on to become a U.S. senator and President Warren Harding's secretary of the interior and the central figure in the Teapot Dome scandal of the 1920s.

2. José Francisco Chaves. The grandson of a territorial governor, Chaves was a prominent political figure—Chaves County in southeastern New Mexico is named for him. Chaves, like Fountain, was a Civil War vet, legislator,

proponent of statehood, and attorney who fought cattle rustlers who died under mysterious circumstances. On November 26, 1904, Chaves was dining with friends at Pinos Wells in south Torrance County. As he was passing a platter of potatoes, according to historian Marc Simmons, Chaves was shot and killed by someone outside the house.

His killer was never brought to justice, although a horse thief named Domingo Valles once confessed. Valles was never tried for the crime. Who killed Chaves? Political foes? A man like Valles whom he'd prosecuted? Was Chaves's death connected with Fountain's? Conspiracy buffs would surely note that both men received threats from a "death committee" on January 12, 1889. The threats warned both men to get out of Santa Fe within thirty-six hours.

3. Ovida "Cricket" Coogler. The 1949 slaying of this eighteen-year-old Las Cruces waitress remains the state's most infamous unsolved murder. Thanks to a grand jury that refused to be cowed by authorities, it blew open a rat's nest of political corruption that shook the state for years.

Coogler was last seen alive on March 31, 1949; her body was found by rabbit hunters twelve miles south of Las Cruces seventeen days later. Critics felt that Sheriff A. L. "Happy" Apodaca did not seem like a lawman intent on finding the truth, and it soon became clear why. The grand jury investigating the killing learned that Apodaca was responsible for chauffeuring political bigwigs when they came to town—and procuring young women as escorts to illegal gambling joints. Apodaca refused to send Coogler's body to El Paso for an autopsy, and before she was buried, someone put one-hundred pounds of quicklime in the casket, destroying all forensic evidence.

One suspect, Jerry Nuzum, a student at the local university and later a running back with the Pittsburgh Steelers, was arrested and tried for the murder. A witness saw Coogler leave the bar with Nuzum. The two appeared to quarrel for a moment, and then Nuzum scooped her into his arms and tried to put her in his car. Coogler resisted and walked away. But a farmer testified that he saw Coogler several hours after the Nuzum incident and that she had gotten into a car—not Nuzum's—with state-government license plates. Another "suspect," a black man named Wesley Byrd, was taken to the desert and tortured by Apodaca, State Police Chief Hubert Beasley, and a deputy. Byrd refused to confess, and the three lawmen served time in prison after being convicted of violating Byrd's civil rights—it was the first time, according to the documentary *The Silence of Cricket Coogler*, that police were convicted of violence against a black man.

A state corporation commissioner, Dan Sedillo, was indicted on moral charges for his alleged involvement with Coogler. On the night of the murder, Sedillo, according to the documentary, was in Las Cruces with Lieutenant Governor Joseph Montoya, later elected to the U.S. Senate. Sedillo was never convicted; all of the witnesses invoked their right against self-incrimination. The grand jury never determined a motive for Coogler's murder or named a killer.

Steve Terrell is a longtime Santa Fe journalist who covers the state legislature and rock and roll for The Santa Fe New Mexican.

HIPPIES AND HOPPER
The Superstar of the Taos Counterculture

Word had spread around America about the communes of Taos, experimental communities with colorful names like New Buffalo, Morning Star East, the Hog Farm and Lama. A tiny town in northern New Mexico, Taos had become a major destination for 1960s dropouts and by the late 1960s, it was hard to walk across the Taos plaza without encountering a cluster of hippies. Still, as of May 23, 1968, the hippies remained something of a mystery to Taos's old-timers.

"Do they smoke pot and raise grass? Are they LSD-lovers instead of love-lovers? Has flower-power turned into cross-eyed glowering?" wondered *The Taos News* in an editorial entitled "The Hippie Problem." As the summer of 1968 approached, the smock-wearing, longhaired newcomers were becoming less of an enigma every day. To the dismay of many locals, scores of hippies were trekking to Taos, population 3,000. Locals had plenty to observe of this strange new breed, and for some Taoseños, familiarity bred contempt. By the end of 1968, any Taoseños who couldn't stomach hippies would have been best advised to leave town, because the worst was yet to come.

As signaled by another article in the May 23 *Taos News*, a hippie tidal wave was about to hit northern New Mexico. A four-paragraph news brief announced the arrival of a Hollywood crew to shoot footage for a film "concerning the travels of two young men across the United States and their encounters and impressions." Within a year, that film, *Easy Rider,* had become a phenomenon, shattering box office records and rewriting the

Hollywood rulebook. The film is an anthem for a generation of disillusioned youth and spends much of its time in Taos's hippie communities, debating the possibilities of a new utopia in the desert. Many viewers identified with Dennis Hopper, the film's messianic, charismatic writer-director-star. Some even packed their rucksacks and headed to New Mexico. *Easy Rider* was about to make life harder for the locals who wanted to keep Taos to themselves.

Hopper had enthusiastically agreed to direct the antiestablishment motorcycle movie Peter Fonda wished to shoot in New Mexico. *Easy Rider* was finished for under $500,000; some of the money went to hallucinogens, and some to the bodyguards Fonda hired to protect himself from Hopper and his violent temper. In the film, which follows two drug dealers biking across America for a final score, Hopper highlights the perceived landmarks of a crumbling society — the mindless racism and violence, the greed, the wasted lives.

Historians Seth Cagin and Philip Dray described *Easy Rider* as a "cautionary fable for hippies," and the film certainly is less than optimistic about the reinvention of American society. In one Taos scene, Billy (played by Hopper) and Wyatt (Fonda) watch as hippies plant seeds in barren land. "This is nothing but sand, man," Billy says. "They ain't gonna make it." Wyatt is more upbeat. "They're going to make it. Dig, man. They're going to make it."

His character Billy may have been cynical, but Hopper recognized Taos's utopian possibilities during his two weeks of filming in the region. He returned to Taos for a Christmas vacation in 1969 and decided to use his *Easy Rider* proceeds to purchase the Mabel Dodge Luhan House, a landmark for the American counterculture of the 1920s and 1930s. When he bought the compound in March 1970, Hopper had hopes of following in Luhan's formidable footsteps and initiating a community of radical artists.

During his nine years as owner, the house would become home to a group of talented jewelers and a gathering place for local artists. Hopper also hosted many of his visionary friends — Leonard Cohen, Bob Dylan, George McGovern, Neil Young — and tried to lure more Hollywood moviemaking to town by editing his studio film *The Last Movie* at the Luhan House. But, as it happened, Hopper's Taos years were marked by trouble. In the early

1970s, he found himself at the center of Taos's escalating, sometimes violent tensions: old-timers versus newcomers, free love and drug experimentation versus traditional, staunchly Catholic beliefs.

The rhetoric, as played out in *The Taos News*, grew vicious. "Hippies are thin creatures, and the winds of change they court will surely sweep them away," one editorial declared. "They are hollow creatures, and their outward manifestations smell. . . . They will soon leave Taos, or will be changed by Taos, and there will be no more hippies." Others expressed their frustrations in racial terms.

In a letter to the editor, Gerald Ortiz y Pino asked other Hispanics to "stop being used. We don't have to prove our manhood, our machismo by beating up hippies. Leave that to the impotent Anglo businessmen." Juan de la Rosa resented that young Latinos, who, he said, "never dodge the military draft," were being impugned by "smelly, crazy-eyed pot and LSD ridden draft-dodgers."

One of the worst moments was the cancellation of the annual Taos Fiesta, the town's biggest communal party. Authorities, according to *The Taos News*, were concerned about the "influx of undesirables." The growing divide between newcomers and locals, Hispanics and Anglos probably helped Hopper to realize that survival on a desert commune was more easily said than done, though many other newcomers remained undeterred. The government in 1970 estimated the hippie population in Taos at more than 3,300, matching the population of native Taoseños. Poet Robert Creeley cited the twenty-seven communes in Taos County and called it "the goyim's Israel," and *Parade Magazine* touted Taos as "a leading candidate for the hippie capital of America." Author John Nichols guessed that Taos had fifteen hippies for every resident during the summer of 1970.

While researching his 1972 book *Commune U.S.A.*, Richard Fairfield visited the Taos area and described it as "swarming with hip people," and then detailed what he called "the Taos hippie-hassles" throughout Taos County. "The hippies didn't have much if any money to spend and their presence scared off all the well-heeled citizens of America who were willing to pay well for their vacations." And, he added, "the authorities decided to harass the [Five Star] commune, and they continued to do so until they had forced it to close." Fairfield visited "The Family," a commune of fifty-four people (twenty-three women, twenty-two men and nine children) who participated in a "group marriage" in a four-room Taos house.

In the spring of 1970, Hopper returned to Taos from Peru, where he had shot *The Last Movie,* and found that the tensions between hippies and locals had escalated into violence. In April 1970 alone, hippies' vehicles were bombed, a bridge to a commune was burned, and bullets were fired into houses. One commune member was shot in the leg. Local leaders even formed a group, the Society for the Preservation of Taos (SPOT), to combat the hippie invasion. One former SPOT member, speaking on conditions of anonymity, said the hippies' lifestyles "turned my stomach. . . . These people hadn't bathed for months, and their ideals were very much opposite of what the community was about. This was a predominately Catholic community, and we were opposed to many of the things the hippies stood for, communes and free love and all of that."

As a symbol of the counterculture and a self-described "freak movie star," Hopper said he found himself frequently confronted by angry Taoseños. "I had a lot of trouble at first from the local Spanish, who didn't want to see an influx of Anglos, especially hippies," he told *The New Yorker* in 1970. "There's a lot of violence. Not abstract violence, like in the big cities, where you read about it in the paper. Out here, when somebody gets shot, you know the person who got shot, you know the guy who shot him, and you know why he shot him."

Hopper began carrying weapons to protect himself from the local teens (he alleged they were beating and raping the hippies with the police's cooperation). On June 16, 1970, Hopper was arrested for holding six young Taoseños at gunpoint; he said police snuck him out a back door of the jail when lynch mobs gathered outside. (Hopper had already been arrested in May for a hit-and-run accident; for this incident, the police charged him with assault with a deadly weapon.) In her book *Dennis Hopper: A Madness to His Method*, Elena Rodriguez quotes Hopper describing the day he stormed Taos High School with his brother David. According to the book, Hopper jumped onstage and faced the students. "Look, I'm here and here I'm going to stay. What's more, there are more freaks coming in over the next few months, and though they may have long hair, they are not the love generation. They're back from Vietnam, and they're hard dudes. They will have weapons—like these." With that, the Hopper brothers flashed their guns. Afterward, Hopper said, the troublemakers left him alone.

Though that oft-repeated tale is a wild one (and the principal of the high school insisted it never happened), the atmosphere in Taos was such that it seems only a few degrees shy of unbelievable. What is true is that by the summer of 1970 Hopper had recruited friends and lined the roof of the Luhan House with automatic weapons. From certain angles, Taos began to look like a war zone.

Hopper believed for a time that he could help bridge the gap between hippie and Hispanic, but, according to Nichols, he ended up exacerbating it. "Dennis first arrived with credentials of being a politically aware person, who was going to help local people articulate their grievances," said Nichols, who chronicled the era in *The New Mexico Review*. "But he was so unstable, so involved in drug tripping, that he became a liability rather than a savior, to put it kindly." According to Rodriguez's book, Hopper's pro-drug testimony before the state legislature didn't help matters.

Hopper's film career collapsed after the failure of *The Last Movie*, and his behavior, fueled by drug and alcohol abuse, became increasingly bizarre. His negative reputation with women also grew (one ex-girlfriend, a Taos native, described him as a "sick pervert"). His short-lived marriages with musician Michelle Phillips (for eight days in 1970) and actress Daria Halprin (for two years, beginning in 1972) probably didn't endear him to his devout neighbors, nor did footage in the documentary *American Dreamer* (1971) showing him in bed with eighteen women.

Nonetheless, in some ways, Hopper was treated as a regular Taoseño. *The Taos News*'s society page described the Hopper-Phillips wedding, with its "150 burning candles" and the bride's "dress of multi-toned green and pink floral print." (The article didn't make note that the officiant, Bruce Conner, was also a legendary avant-garde filmmaker and artist.) Hopper annually opened his art-filled house to the public. On one occasion, according to the society page, Mrs. Sue McCleery presided over the punch bowl and Hopper showed everyone clips from *The Last Movie*.

Perhaps the regular-guy treatment Hopper received in Taos helped him stick it out there. After selling the Luhan House in 1978, he bought and renovated the El Cortez theater. With his career on steadier ground (he was nominated for an Oscar for his 1986 role in *Hoosiers*), Hopper now lives closer to Hollywood, in Venice, California, but periodically visits the property he owns in Taos.

As it turns out, Hopper has left a positive mark on some locals, especially through his active participation in the Taos art scene. Like Mabel Dodge Luhan, he lured many major countercultural figures to Taos, and championed the work of numerous local artists, including conceptual artist Ron Cooper. "What was interesting to me about Dennis was, regardless of whatever kind of emotional state he was in, he was first and foremost really interested in art," Cooper said. "He lives and breathes it, whether he is in Hollywood or Taos."

And, in a strange way, many appreciated the trouble Hopper caused. He was, after all, a true maverick, the kind of man that New Mexicans respect, at least in hindsight. "He raised a lot of hell and bothered a lot of people when he got to partying," said John Mingenbach, who lives next to the Luhan House. "There were midnight shootings of Browning automatic rifles, silly stuff that doesn't have much place in a community this tightly packed. But he mixed very well when he wanted to, and in retrospect, after he left, we realized how much fun he was to have around."

SPOTLIGHT:
PETER FONDA'S LOST WESTERN

Two years after *Easy Rider*, Peter Fonda returned to New Mexico to direct and star in *The Hired Hand*, the story of a cowboy who comes home to his wife and farm after seven years of roaming. After a brief, badly publicized release—the film lasted in theaters for just two weeks —*The Hired Hand* disappeared.

In 2003, *The Hired Hand*'s editor Frank Mazzola presented a restored version of the film at festivals, and it began to find a new generation of admirers. The film critic Amy Taubin, writing in *ArtForum*, described it in flattering terms: "Combining a classic genre (the Western) with a markedly personal directorial approach, realistic characters with a mystical devotion to the land, and meticulous craft with a touch of visual and aural experimentation, it is as much an independent-film prototype as *Easy Rider*." Among the film's other fans was Clint Eastwood, who cited as it a central influence on his Oscar-winning *Unforgiven*.

In 2003, the Sundance Channel broadcast *The Hired Hand* and released it on DVD, providing a missing piece of New Mexico's film history. In addition to offering gorgeous footage of the state, the poetic, idiosyncratic movie is part of a long tradition of unconventional Westerns shot in New Mexico. The 1929 film *Redskin* offered a rare sympathetic look at Native people; the Anthony Mann-James Stewart *The Man from Laramie* was edgy and far from idealistic about the American frontier; and *Lonely Are the Brave*, adapted from an Edward Abbey story, injects modern machines and culture into the story of an aging cowpoke.

Here are some excerpts from an interview I conducted with Peter Fonda prior to a screening of *The Hired Hand* at the 2003 Taos Talking Picture Festival.

How big of a role did New Mexico play in the film? How did you find all of those locations?

New Mexico was the first place I went looking for *Hired Hand* locations. We went around and saw the possible Western streets. At one point we stopped—my cameraman Vilmos Zsigmond, the assistant director, somebody from the New Mexico film agency—at a little store. They had some stuff in pawn, and I bought a belt, and was leafing through a book and saw the perfect place. The [shopkeeper] knew it, told me how to get there. It was Cabezon, an abandoned town, and it was the first location we secured. We knew that would be our beginning and ending of the film.

You got a lot of diversity out of one state—rivers, mountains, those huge open spaces—everything but that Western street later shot on MGM's back lot.

We spent an interesting second-unit dash through the state with horses—the sheriff that was with us didn't know what to do, especially when we cut fence. We cut the horses out so we could ride across this big great briny body of water—that didn't get into the film. But then we repaired the fence and moved along. [New Mexico] became part of the story. I like to make the background in the film another character, a full character. [The locations] determine so much of what happens . . . and that state offers more character in its scenic backgrounds than any other state. There are many different tastes. . . . [And] it was far enough away from the studio executives that they had to make special efforts to get to it.

Can you tell me the story of your stalker?

A kid came to my room at the Inn of the Governors carrying Kahil Gibran's *The Prophet* under his arm. He said, "Tell me what to do, you are the only one who can tell me what to do." So I told him, "You've got to tell them all the truth." He said okay and marched out of the room. That's the last time I thought I'd see him.

[In Cabezon], which is a nineteen-mile run from the highway on dirt road . . . he showed up on the set. I was at the far end of the town shooting the jail sequence when one of the players, Ted Marklin, who looked similar to me, came down. He was very nervous. Apparently the dude had come up to Teddy, thinking he was me, and said, "I have to kill you and take care of your wife and children, too, but I can't do it now because the sun and the moon are in the sky at the same time."

The New Mexico State Police took the kid to the border and threw him into Arizona and told him not to come back, and they assigned a deputy to me. [The deputy] sat in his car outside this hippie-run, beautiful hot springs [Jemez, where the cast and crew stayed]. He'd never come in. We'd say, "Come on in, have some food, it's really good, all homemade, all natural." "No, I'll stay here." I never did get him to have a meal with me, but he at least did his job. Nobody threatened to kill me again.

You obviously love the skies here. And the film gives a great sense of how wild New Mexico was, even in the early 1970s.

Someone once said there were more sunsets in *The Hired Hand* than in any other movie. I didn't know if that was a compliment or not, but I did indeed shoot a lot of sunsets. I know I can always go back to New Mexico and shoot any other film that needs outside space, a Western look, with mountains and rivers.

THE GHOST IN THE HALL
Cimarron's Haunted Hotel

Sometime around 1902, when he was fifteen, Fred Lambert and his brother counted every bullet hole in the ceiling of the Lambert Inn, where he lived. There were more than 400 of them, most of which, the Lamberts guessed, were ceremonial. Someone shot off his gun to celebrate something — maybe the birth of a child, or, much more likely, a winning poker hand. But in a place like the Lambert, now called the St. James Hotel, many of the holes would have been carved by angry bullets. In fact, there have been twenty-six murders in the hotel, and Lambert, a painter, amateur historian, and the son of St. James founder Henry Lambert, eventually documented them all.

Forget the O.K. Corral. Forget Dodge City and Tombstone. Cimarron, New Mexico, with its central watering hole and stopover, the St. James Hotel, was as wild as any Wild West town in the late 1800s. Filled with outlaws and gunfighters, cowboys and miners, cowards and heroes, this was a place where the scales of justice could be easily tipped by a quick trigger finger. How violent was the town? Even a string of quiet days became newsworthy: "Everything is quiet in Cimarron," the *Las Vegas Gazette* reported in the 1870s. "Nobody has been killed for three days."

Today, visitors to sleepy Cimarron, population 900, are much more likely to quick draw a credit card than a six-shooter. Quiet for much of the year, the town buzzes each summer and fall with Boy Scouts (as many as 25,000 of them annually camp out at the nearby Philmont Scout Ranch) and hunters. Those who visit the town, located fifty miles east of Taos, nearly always stop at the St. James, a monument to a livelier, and deadlier, time.

The hallways and rooms at the St. James are filled with remnants of the old West: worn Victorian couches, photos of cowboy heroes, even an antique roulette wheel. One wall holds a handmade plaque honoring the outlaw Clay Allison — it calls him "the Gentleman Gunfighter," and lists his nineteen victims, including an "unknown Mexican," "five Negro soldiers," and "three Negro soldiers."

As many as 10,000 called Cimarron home during its heyday, from around 1850 to 1910. It was the capital of the biggest piece of private property in the history of the United States — the Maxwell Land Grant. Overseen by Lucien Maxwell, Cimarron's benign feudal lord, the grant encompassed 1.7 million acres, more than three Rhode Islands. Ranching ruled the day, but some also found profit in mining (especially during a brief gold rush).

Henry Lambert charted a different course. In 1871, the French-born maverick (a former personal chef to General Ulysses S. Grant) bought an existing saloon and some empty land for about $200. He spent $17,000 expanding the building into a hotel, an appropriate place, Lambert figured, to make his fortune, and also to raise a family. His boy Fred, born upstairs (during a cyclone, according to old-timers), was tending bar by age thirteen and had seen enough action by age fifteen to qualify for a lawman's badge.

Renegades including Blackjack Ketchum and Daniel Boone II were St. James regulars. Governor Lew Wallace penned part of his *Ben Hur* at the hotel; legendary cowboy novelist Zane Grey also wrote at the St. James; and Frederic Remington painted the nearby hills. Buffalo Bill Cody and Annie Oakley — at least according to legend — planned their Wild West shows from the saloon, and Tom Thumb and Thumbelina stopped in. Wyatt Earp, Doc Holliday, Bat Masterson, and Jesse James were said to have visited. And Davy Crockett's unmarked grave, according to legend, sits in a Cimarron cemetery not far from Henry Lambert's final resting place.

Some of those who spent their final night at the St. James don't rest so easily. Many say the ghosts of several former guests haunt the place.

Cimarron resident Marjorie Munden, who worked at the hotel in the 1980s, describes run-ins with a prankster ghost, who rearranged piles of credit card slips. "I don't do the ghost thing—I was not a believer," she said. "But this was definitely a ghostly experience." Perry Champion, the hotel's current manager and chef, once woke up when he felt someone pulling his head into the air, only to find himself alone in the room. He also once saw a kitchen knife launch itself into the air. "I consider myself a pretty pragmatic guy—a skeptic," he said. "That started me on the road to believing."

Former owner Ed Sitzberger said the ghosts remain more mischievous than malicious, but his ex-wife butted heads with a hostile spirit. After she demanded that the ghost of gunslinger T. J. Wright leave the hotel, "she saw a swirling in the corner," Sitzberger reported, "and it knocked her down. She got out of the way when it came back. After that, she stayed clear of that room." That room, number 18, remains closed to the public. What's more, every few days, hotel staff, after giving a superstitious knock, enter the room and refill T.J.'s shot glasses with Jack Daniels. (Some say Wright drains each shot; Champion suspects evaporation.)

Everyone's favorite ghost is Mary Lambert, Henry's beloved wife. She leaves her musty rose scent in otherwise empty rooms, and has been known to swipe guests' perfume and fiddle with Ouija boards. Mary, T.J., and the others have provided enough paranormal activity to lure TV shows, including *Unsolved Mysteries* and *A Current Affair*, to Cimarron.

The attention has helped enliven Cimarron and the St. James, which reopened its rooms in 1985 and now offers a gourmet menu in its café and dining room. The town, through 150 years of ups and downs, seems to have retained a sense of optimism, perhaps best reflected in the words of the *Cimarron Citizen*. The short-lived paper praised the town in its inaugural issue of March 1908: "Being one-half mile from Heaven, we have some of its climate. We have unlimited water, vast forests, untold mineral wealth, fertile grazing and farming lands. In fact, everything but exorbitant tax assessment and the smallpox is to be found at Cimarron."

THE BIG WEEKEND
Santa Fe Indian Market

If you are an artist who has managed to score a booth at Santa Fe Indian Market, the last thing you want to do is oversleep on the first morning. But that's what Annie Antone did. By the time Antone, a basket weaver and member of the Tohono O'odham tribe, arrived in downtown Santa Fe with fellow weaver Leona Antone (no relation), it was after 8:00 a.m., and the streets were jammed. Parking spaces were gone. As they jostled their way to their booth, the Antones realized that Indian Market isn't your typical, leisurely paced art fair.

On opening day of the market, which falls on a Saturday each August, an estimated 70,000 visitors descend on Santa Fe, shopping for pots, jewelry, weavings, sculpture, and paintings by artists from around the country (in 2004, there were 1,100 artists from 100 tribes). Over the course of the weekend, Native artists, many of whom work in isolation during the year, get the superstar treatment.

"There were people waiting there for us to show up," Antone said of her first market morning. "We said, 'Wow!' I'd never seen that before. I'd only sold our weavings through traders, and had never even met buyers. I was surprised that so many people would line up to buy our work."

No one knows the exact amount of money that changes hands at Indian Market — artists and collectors deal directly with each other — but it's not unusual to see handcrafted pieces of jewelry and pots selling for as much as $10,000. Some prizewinning pieces go for still more. In 2002, a first-place pot by Lonnie Vigil of Nambé Pueblo went for an estimated

$30,000, and a car painted by Dan Namingha, and accessorized by nine other Native artists, sold at a fund-raiser for $90,000.

But the market has influence beyond the money exchanged. Collectors and curators from Japan, Italy, Germany, and Australia take the artifacts and ideas they find there home. Producers of other events study Indian Market's model. Even the U.S. Postal Service has taken notice — it launched its Art of the American Indian stamp series at the 2004 market. Thanks in part to Indian Market, the importance of indigenous art is embraced around the world.

Many artists have launched international reputations from their market booths. That list includes Teri Greeves (Kiowa); Navajo potter Harrison Begay Jr.; Navajo jewelers Perry Shorty and Jesse Monongye; the radical art-making brothers Diego and Mateo Romero (a painter and potter, respectively, from Cochiti); and the jewelry team of Gail Bird (Santo Domingo-Laguna) and Yazzie Johnson (Navajo).

Each year, the 500 so-called "tenured" artists can stake a claim on a booth; everyone else competes for space by sending slides to a jury of curators assembled by the Southwestern Association for Indian Arts (SWAIA). The producer of Indian Market, SWAIA oversees a very selective process. Hundreds of artists won't make the cut. The chosen ones bring their works to Santa Fe, where, the night before the market opens, a jury evaluates them.

More than 300 works win ribbons, and $60,000 in prize money is distributed in several categories, including jewelry, pottery, painting, sculpture, textiles, and clothing. On Saturday, things get crazy. Most artists will arrive no later than 6:00 a.m. to set up their booths, and some find collectors already lined up. The most intrepid buyers camp out in the booths of their favorite artists, trying to sleep while the revelry of market weekend swirls around them. By the time Indian Market officially opens at 7:00 a.m. Saturday, eager buyers have surrounded many booths, and aspiring artists and curiosity seekers mill about.

Those serious about collecting Native art will wait, often a dozen deep, to purchase and study the works and to meet the artists. Before breakfast, buzz about hot items and artists has bounced across the Santa Fe plaza and back several times. By mid-morning on Saturday, many of the ribbon-winning artists will have sold all of their work.

Some artists, thanks in part to the financial incentives, spend a good portion of the year gearing up for the market. "This is the Olympics of Indian art and the Indian Oscars rolled into one," said Marcus Amerman, a Santa Fe-based Choctaw bead worker, painter, and sculptor who has shown his work at the market since the mid-1980s. "I know a lot of artists in the Southwest who can afford to make it because of their earnings at Indian Market."

Amerman himself is one example. He has won ribbons in a variety of categories, including three Artists' Choice awards, and dedicates much of his time to working on new pieces for the upcoming market or commissions lined up at the previous one.

Jamie Okuma, a twenty-seven-year-old Luiseno Shoshone-Bannock doll maker, first exhibited her detailed beaded dolls at the 1997 market. By the 2000 Indian Market, she had begun to lose confidence in her future as an artist. Then she got the news: her doll had been chosen from more than 1,000 pieces—every piece of art entered, including jewelry, pottery, paintings, textiles, and sculpture—as the winner of the Best of Show ribbon.

"I had been considering a career change, maybe becoming a graphic designer," Okuma said. "But once I won that award, it changed everything. I sold out that year and every year since. I wouldn't have had a career without Indian Market." Okuma has proven to be something of a prodigy, winning Best of Show again in 2002, a remarkable feat for a young woman competing against close to 1,000 seasoned artists. Her pieces sell for the price of a new car.

Many artists, even the most successful, continue to return to Indian Market every year. Over the years, the famed Santo Domingo potter Robert Tenorio has developed an eve-of-market ritual: he lines up all of his pots and spends some time saying goodbye. Then he folds each in a Pendleton blanket using a technique—"the old Santo Domingo wrap"—that leaves a handy knot at the top. After a few hours of sleep, he'll load his pots into his van and at around 2:00 or 3:00 a.m. drive this precious cargo to the Santa Fe plaza.

It's not a long trip. Santo Domingo Pueblo to downtown Santa Fe takes less than an hour, but Tenorio said that it can feel like a big deal. It wasn't always that way. As recently as the mid-1960s, Tenorio will tell you, Indian Market was just another day, except for the prize ribbons.

"You wouldn't have to enter, or pick out your best works and take them to the judges," said Tenorio, who helped his family sell jewelry under the portal at the Palace of the Governors. "The judges would just walk around, and judge what was available to look at."

The archaeologist Edgar Lee Hewett, a founder of the School of American Research, launched what was then called the Southwest Indian Fair and Arts and Crafts Exhibitions in 1922. He intended to create a showcase that would ensure the continuance of Native art forms. If Native potters could earn their keep by making pots, he reasoned, then pots would continue to be made. Helping Native people rescue and perpetuate their lifeways may sound sensible today, but in the 1920s, it was a radical concept, according to Bruce Bernstein, assistant director for cultural resources at the Smithsonian's National Museum of the American Indian.

"It was a revelation for Native people after being degraded and demeaned by the European population—suddenly there is an interest in their culture and their lives. [Non-Natives] were even paying Native artists for their pots," said Bernstein, who serves as a board member of SWAIA.

At the beginning of the market, the quality of art surprised many, even writers in the center of so-called "Indian Country." In 1922, *The Santa Fe New Mexican* wrote:

> We call these people "untutored," and yet, to watch a desert dweller spill varicolored sands between his fingers into a magic pattern on the ground glowing with color and beauty; to see rich designs springing from under the flying fingers of a Navajo woman seated impassive before her loom; to see the cunning of the silversmith; enigmatic pictures evolving in beads and straw, sheer beauty flowing from the finger tips of this strange race of men and women, to study their symbolism and listen to their age-old tradition, is to be lost in wonder.

Bernstein describes Indian Market as the engine in the evolution and preservation of Southwestern Native artistic practices from its very beginning. "The Indian Fair in 1922 became the vehicle for new styles of pottery and the idea of selling pottery to the non-Indian world," Bernstein said. "This wasn't selling pots by the roadside for nickels and dimes, but real art pottery."

After a hiatus, the event was recast in 1936 as Indian Market. The new manager, Maria Chabot, gave more autonomy to the artists, allowing them to set prices and sell directly to the buyers. The direct sales, though worrisome to tax collectors, have remained an essential feature of each market since.

"What SWAIA and Indian Market do is to set the table," said former SWAIA director Jai Lakshman. "We provide the forum and space. We are really just a vehicle for the art and artists." Thanks in part to Indian Market, Native art has increasingly found its way into fine-art museums and galleries outside of the Southwest.

The list of Native artists who have graduated from the market to museums include Ramona Sakiestewa, Nora Naranjo Morse, Roxanne Swentzell, Pablita Velarde, Geronima Montoya, and Bob Haozous. Market isn't every artist's ultimate goal. Some tire of carrying their own work, setting up their own booths, and the early wake-up calls and circus-like atmosphere associated with Market. Navajo artist and writer Shonto Begay believes the market's focus on art as commodity can overwhelm its value as sacred object. Indian Market rewards the conventional, he said, not the daring or innovative.

"You can see plenty of people who made works at the last minute to satisfy the market requirements," said Begay, author of *Navajo: Voices and Visions Across the Mesa* and *Ma' II and Cousin Horned Toad.* "I get a bit cynical about market, because it in some ways keeps our art and people marginalized. Take the choice of poster. Every year, the market poster is a soulless, pretty picture . . . something easily swallowed by the tourists, with feathers and beads and colorful horses and stoic Indians. This is what we are sometimes made to believe Indian art is. The standards of Indian Market help perpetuate that. . . . People come to my booth, look at my paintings and say, 'That's not Indian.'"

But even Begay readily acknowledges how important Indian Market has been in its support of Native artists. Having a booth at Indian Market can legitimate an artist, and bring plenty of financial reward.

"Market is a chance to immerse friends and family in the passion you have been immersed in for the whole year," Begay said. "For that weekend, my relatives know that being an artist is a job, not just messing around and starving. . . . The third week in August, we artists make sure our trucks are running."

Norma Howard, a Choctaw-Chickasaw watercolor painter, makes the long drive to Santa Fe from Stigler, Oklahoma, each August (her first Indian Market was also her first trip west of Oklahoma City). By the end of a day at market, Howard said her mind is too filled with ideas to go to sleep—she'll head back to the hotel and start in on a new canvas. Howard is one of many who credits Indian Market with jump-starting her career. In Oklahoma, she said, art making was seen by most as a hobby. By the end of her first Indian Market, she thought of herself as a professional.

"I'd go to a few shows around Oklahoma, but it's hard to make a living doing art there," said Howard, who won a best-of-division ribbon in 2003. "Allan Houser said that if he had lived in Oklahoma he would have starved. You have to go where people enjoy your work and where you can make a living. That happens at the Indian Market. . . . You see everyone's best work, and it makes you want to show your best. If I make a good painting in September, I'll set it aside until August so I can show it first at Santa Fe. . . . When the summer comes, I'll get the rush of adrenaline: 'I've got three more months, two more months.' When it gets close, I don't rest. I don't think many artists do."

Reunions abound each August. Lonnie Vigil, a Nambé Pueblo potter, hosts an annual feast and preview of his works on the eve of market at his house and studio in Nambé. Once a Washington, D.C.-based financial analyst with the U.S. government, Vigil discovered his talent for making pottery relatively late in life, in his thirties. At his first Indian Market in 1990, he received three awards. It was a momentous occasion for Vigil and Nambé Pueblo, which had seen its pottery-making traditions all but disappear.

Bernstein said that this type of phenomenon demonstrates the power of Indian Market. "One of Lonnie's pots is named Best of Show by a panel of judges who know what they are doing," said Bernstein, who has been researching and writing about Indian Market for more than twenty years, "so then the pot sells right away, the value of it increases, and people take notice of it." In large part because of the attention they've received at Indian Market, Vigil's pots have gone on to be exhibited in such museums as the Smithsonian, the Museum of Fine Arts in Boston, and the American Craft Museum, and are part of the private collections of Bill and Hillary Clinton and the Dalai Lama.

For many non-Natives, as Bernstein points out, the market provides an opportunity to discuss Native art and culture with Native people. That's because the artists run their own booths—no middlemen split the profits here. For a non-Native to walk from booth to booth talking to artists can be a radicalizing experience.

"Native art, like all art forms, is about people's lives and cultures," Bernstein said. "One of the most encouraging elements of the success of Native art is that it continues to inform us about Native people—their histories, who they are today, and how they are changing."

Indian Market once had rigorous rules about what was "traditional" art, and therefore deserved a spot, and what wasn't. Those rules have been relaxed over the years, and a more vibrant and fluid definition of Native art has begun to emerge. Today, the market does the same for a wide array of media and forms of expression. That's one reason Hopi potter Rondina Huma, one of the most respected Native artists, has returned each of the past thirty years. She fully expects to see and learn something new.

"I didn't know there was this much talent out there in the whole world," said Huma, who won Best of Show ribbons in 1986 and 1996 for her intricate, dazzlingly designed pots. "It's exciting to be with so many talented people, especially the young artists."

While artists like Huma might learn from younger artists, plenty of emerging painters, sculptors, potters, and jewelers use Indian Market as an opportunity to study the works of their elders. Huma hopes to teach two of her grandchildren to follow in her path. Norma Howard's son Daniel, also a painter, first participated in Market in 2004.

Daryl Whitegeese, a former electrical engineer, is the grandson of the legendary Santa Clara potter Margaret Tafoya and son of 2003 Indian Market Best of Show winner Lu Ann Tafoya. For his first thirty-eight years,

Whitegeese never considered becoming a potter, even though he enjoyed listening to his mother and grandmother talk about their work. In 2002, he finally gave pottery a try, was accepted into the market and won a ribbon. He took home an award in 2003 for excellence in traditional arts.

"Becoming an artist is something I never thought would happen," said Whitegeese, who creates small, perfectly proportioned pots. "It didn't seem like my path in life. But I'm proud to be part of Indian Market, and proud to be there with my mom. Last year, I was looking at one of the magazines that had a list of who won which prize. I saw my mom's name and right there in the next column was my name. That really makes me feel good."

Whitegeese plans on returning each year, and so does Navajo sculptor Larry Yazzie, who has participated since 1986 and won numerous ribbons, including the best sculpture award in 2002. "I look at the Indian Market as a kind of drinking pool," explains Yazzie. "Everyone gets thirsty and needs to drink. You can't live without it. If you are an Indian artist, Indian Market is the place you need to be."

THE RISE OF PUBLIC ART
The WPA Comes to New Mexico

"My God, she has six fingers!" said Emil Bisttram, surveying his work. And so she did, she being a woman in Bisttram's mural, painted in a courthouse in Taos. As described in a 1934 *Taos Valley News* article entitled "Artist Produces Freak in Court House," Bisttram had painted a subject with "four fingers closed, one finger pointing up, and a thumb beside." And so Bisttram took out his brushes, ready to do the anatomically correct thing and fix the woman's hand.

Okay, so the WPA wasn't perfect. Still, Bisttram's fresco, commissioned as part of a New Deal program known as the Works Progress Administration (WPA), was part of a truly remarkable moment in American art. Through this program, initiated by President Franklin Delano Roosevelt, the United States demonstrated the possibilities of artists and the government working together. The WPA's projects combined federal funds, public spaces, and talented artists to transform our nation's relationship to the arts.

The WPA, Roosevelt's $5 billion employment plan, passed Congress in 1935 and included the federal art, theater, music and writers programs. Through these projects the U.S. government kept nearly 40,000 artists, writers, and performers working during the Great Depression. Along the way, the federal funds led to a dazzlingly diverse body of work, which radically altered the way Americans see, make, display, contextualize, and fund all kinds of art, from theater to painting, furniture making to photography. Some historians go so far as to argue that the works of art created under the New Deal programs served as a foundation of a true national identity. Alfred Kazin called the New Deal works "the literature of nationhood" that offered an entirely new way to understand what it meant to be American.

In New Mexico, the WPA programs had especially powerful effects. Would-be painters, writers, and sculptors suddenly had salaries, viable projects, and mentors. More established artists, like Bisttram (who trained as a muralist with Diego Rivera), could set aside the worries of the marketplace to work on projects they believed in passionately. Over the course of just a few years, the public perception grew: art and artists could be essential parts of a vibrant community. From Alamogordo to Wagon Mound, New Mexico's artists created work that could speak to their neighbors' struggles and hopes. Tiny villages with limited access to art suddenly were able to watch some of the state's most gifted artists sketch and render beautiful murals or sculptures.

"The 1930s was the first time that many people had seen art in person," said Kathryn Flynn, a former New Mexico deputy secretary of state and the author of the WPA book *Treasures on New Mexico Trails*. "Many had only seen reproductions, on calendars, for example. And it was the first time many saw an artist at work, doing murals on public buildings, and the first time they could visit with and talk to an artist. I think they found out artists were human beings, just like the rest of us."

Through her Santa Fe-based organization, the National New Deal Preservation Association, Flynn hopes to spread the good word nationwide. The organization already has helped raise consciousness about the value of Depression-era art in New Mexico (the ten Taos courthouse frescoes, which had suffered for years thanks to a leaky roof, are among the lucky works to have been rescued).

But what did WPA art look like? It's a bit hard to characterize, since the WPA's art-making mission was an inclusive one. "American art is anything an American artist does," the Federal Art Program director Holger Cahill once said. That policy significantly benefited New Mexico's artists. A wood carver like Patrocio Barela, described by *Time* magazine in 1936 as the "discovery of the year," found himself suddenly, and justifiably, elevated from mere craftsman to the exalted category of artist. Barela was among the numerous New Mexicans whose work toured the country, included in exhibitions in New York, Chicago, and Washington, D.C.

Those exhibits helped establish the Spanish colonial style as an important American art form.

The WPA supported and nurtured some of the icons of New Mexico art: Kenneth Adams, Pop Chalee, Allan Houser, Gustave Baumann, Gene Kloss, William Lumpkins, Maria Martinez, Will Shuster, and Pablita Velarde among them. It also left an essential structural legacy. Historian Guillermo Lux notes that the annual Spanish Market, one of New Mexico's biggest art events, began as WPA-designed sales on the plaza. And Flynn lists hundreds of WPA works still publicly displayed.

Another important WPA element, more recently discovered, is the photography from the Farm Security Administration (FSA). Through this New Deal program, photographers, including John Collier Jr. and Russell Lee, created a striking document of an unseen New Mexico. Sent to capture the state's flavor ("Don't forget that the burro is an important part of that agriculture," his boss Roy Stryker wired him from Washington. "We could stand quite a few shots of the little animal"), Lee discovered Pie Town, a struggling village of homesteaders. The Pie Town photos, as well as Collier's photos of the tiny northern New Mexico communities Peñasco, Questa, and Trampas have become photographic icons.

The WPA meant more to New Mexico than murals and paintings. The arts accounted for a mere 5 percent of the total WPA budget. Roads, post offices, and other public buildings (including the Albuquerque Little Theater, the Bandelier buildings, and the Santa Fe Public Library) were built with federal monies. By one estimate, more than half of New Mexicans were on the federal payroll at some time during the 1930s.

Nationally, the projects encouraged a huge range of expressive and community-building activities. An estimated fourteen million pupils took music classes, courtesy of the New Deal. New Deal funding helped launch national oral-history and folklore-studies movements, with recordists fanning out across the country to capture the stories and songs of real Americans. Through the Federal Writers Program (whose roster included Richard Wright, Saul Bellow, Ralph Ellison, John Cheever, Studs Terkel, and Zora Neale Hurston), a series of guidebooks and literary magazines were published. The New Mexico guidebook, completed in 1941, remains one of the best books on the state.

But it is on the New Deal's visual-arts component that so many look back with nostalgia and even a bit of awe. Though the Great Depression was among the worst of times for Americans, it may well have been the best of times for American art. A steady stream of books and exhibits celebrating the period continue to be published. What's a bit surprising is how unpopular the New Deal arts programs were while they were actually under way. It wasn't just the project's startling inefficiency that came under attack (the Scottish word "boondoggle" was imported to the United States to describe the WPA). Instead, the focus was on the politics of the artworks themselves, which by today's standards seem relatively innocuous.

Republican Representative Everett Dirkson of Illinois, who called WPA art "salacious tripe," led tireless legislative campaigns over funding. The House Un-American Activities Committee, now infamous, thanks to its strong-arm tactics in the 1950s under Joseph McCarthy, took shape in 1938 to attack the WPA program. Generally, the focus remained on the artists, described as part of the "Communist menace." Plays from the Federal Theatre Project were especially vulnerable. The John Houseman-Orson Welles production of *The Cradle Will Rock* (the subject of a 1999 Tim Robbins movie) was banned, and became a favorite target. One senator described the New Deal works as coming from "the gutters of the Kremlin."

By the late 1930s, the death knell was ringing for the golden age of American public art. Having survived years of massive cuts, the Federal Arts Project officially succumbed in 1943. Today, the U.S. government spends only a tiny fraction of what it did during the New Deal on art. Steve Yates, a curator at the Museum of New Mexico, finds that distressing.

"Back then, there was no money and a lot of support," said Yates, who assembled the 1993 FSA exhibit Threads of Culture for the Museum of Fine Arts in Santa Fe. "Today, there is plenty of money and no support. The economy has been burning up, but simultaneously, there has been the rise of the idea that artists should support themselves like businessmen. I'm not saying that market-driven art is bad and government-funded art is good. What we really need is a balance. Without that balance, you get mediocrity.

"And the art back then was not mediocre—artists were making documents that were universal statements, that reveal the human condition, that explore social issues and individual experiences. There were works that transcend time. And that is what great art does."

SPOTLIGHT:
FIVE FAVORITE WPA WORKS
BY NEW MEXICO ARTISTS
By Kathryn Flynn

1. ***Governor Greets the People*** (Pablita Velarde) In 1939, at age 19, Velarde painted 72 watercolors at Bandelier National Monument, each depicting an aspect of daily life at Santa Clara Pueblo. Velarde remembered the impact of her WPA work: the opportunity helped her become a professional artist and earn enough money to return to Santa Clara Pueblo and build her own home. But tribal elders were not happy with Velarde for exposing some of their customs. This painting is available from the National New Deal Preservation Association (NNDPA) as a license plate, which thrills Velarde: "Now they'll see my art coming and going!"

2. ***Rain Priest*** (Alice Geneva Glasier (Gene) Kloss) Frequently thought to be a man, Taos's Gene Kloss is best known for her fine etchings, including nine different New Mexico scenes that were reproduced and distributed In schools, libraries and universities across New Mexico and in Washington, D.C. Many originals are still hanging in the original thirty-one sites. This colorful oil painting is in the Albuquerque Museum collection.

3. ***The Twelfth Chapter of Ecclesiastes*** (Lloyd Moylan) This large, colorful mural in the Administration Building at Eastern New Mexico University in Portales was the inspiration behind the NNDPA. Moylan also

created large murals at Highlands University and in the Gallup-McKinley County Courthouse, along with numerous smaller paintings. The paint used in this mural was donated from an unknown private individual who selected the subject and stipulated that the artist must not paint on Sunday. When he was caught painting on Sunday, Moylan's response was, "What better day to paint the Lord's Word than on the Lord's Day!"

4. *Mercy* (Oliver LaGrone) The first African American to graduate from the University of New Mexico Art Department was grateful to the WPA for providing him the chance to depict a childhood memory: his mother nursing him through malaria. This uncast sculpture was placed in the lobby at Carrie Tingley Hospital for Crippled Children in Hot Springs (now Truth or Consequences) and the children frequently climbed on it. The sculpture's thumb was replaced many times by the hospital. When the hospital moved to Albuquerque, Dr. LaGrone, then a professor in Pennsylvania, returned to his hometown and created a new thumb for the sculpture.

5. *The Old Cuba Road* (William Penhallow Henderson) This talented man designed and built houses, carved furniture, created theater sets and painted large and small paintings. Six of his finest works can be viewed at the Federal Courthouse in Santa Fe. Henderson came to New Mexico in 1916 because of his wife's poor health (she had tuberculosis) and fell in love with the vast outdoors. For his courthouse creations, Henderson said he wanted to "bring the out-of-doors inside to be enjoyed indoors."

Kathryn Flynn, a former New Mexico deputy secretary of state, is editor of Treasures on New Mexico Trails: Discover New Deal Art and Architecture *(Sunstone Press) and executive director of the National New Deal Preservation Association.*

HAIL TO THE CHIEFS
The Rise of a Basketball Powerhouse

The basketball bounced out of bounds. The Kirtland Central High School Lady Broncos controlled the in-bounds pass. The buzzer sounded. And the Shiprock High School Lady Chieftains were defeated. The two teams had played perhaps the closest game in the history of basketball, tied after one quarter, tied after two quarters, after three quarters, four quarters, and one overtime. But when the second overtime period ended, Shiprock had come up one point short. The Kirtland Central Broncos won the 1987 New Mexico AAA girls basketball championship by a score of 62-61. The girls hoisted the state championship trophy for the eighth straight year, the longest streak in the country. Meanwhile, in the locker room, the Shiprock girls had already decided: next year would be different.

Any Shiprock fan with a decent memory could hardly paint the Chieftains' last-second overtime loss as a disappointment. Only a few years earlier, it would have been hard to imagine the Lady Chieftains being competitive in the championship game. Throughout the late 1970s and most of the 1980s, the Kirtland Lady Broncos were indomitable. Their last loss in the state championship came when Jimmy Carter was president. But in 1983, change had come to Shiprock, in the form of new head coach Jerry Richardson. He was a man who knew a little something about being an underdog. One of a handful of African American students to integrate the previously all-white schools of Texarkana, Texas, Richardson had been a standout high-school basketball star, twice leading the city in scoring. He also excelled in track and field, at which he continued to compete as a student at Northwest Louisiana State. And now he was in Navajo country, a young coach and newcomer with a strategy to defeat what was probably the best girls' basketball team in the United States.

When Richardson arrived, the basketball program he took over simply couldn't compete with Kirtland's finely tuned hoops machine. In Kirtland, located just eighteen miles from Shiprock in New Mexico's Four Corners area, girls grew up dreaming not of becoming actresses or teachers or presidents of the United States but of playing on their high-school basketball team. Those who made the cut adhered to a rigorous, regimented system—a controlled, efficient style of basketball—and won championship after championship.

Initially, Richardson's girls at Shiprock had neither the training nor the discipline necessary to challenge Kirtland. Many of the girls in Shiprock, New Mexico, grew up in dire circumstances. The town had high rates of unemployment, drug and alcohol abuse and other measures of despair. "They were used to losing. They didn't worry about losing," Richardson told filmmaker Rick Derby in a 1989 interview. "I had never been associated with anything that lost. So we had to change some attitudes, to make them more aggressive."

And he did, building a dedicated group of players, led by guards Sheila Smiley and Vernetta Begay and center Natasha Johnson. When forward Cheryl Lee decided to transfer to Shiprock from Kirtland in 1985, the scales seemed to be tipping toward the Chieftains. Lee was an extremely hard worker. It wasn't unusual for her to spend nine hours in the gym, perfecting her shot. Her transfer added fire to the rivalry.

Lee's choice also helped spotlight the racial component of the Chieftain-Bronco feud. Shiprock, a reservation school, had an all-Navajo team. The roster of Kirtland, once a Mormon town, was more ethnically mixed. Some players, Lee among them, felt that the Navajo players on Kirtland's team faced a double standard. "The perception was that the coach favored the Anglo players," Lee told me. "They got the playing time and the press coverage, they signed the letters of intent and received the scholarships. It seemed to me that none of the Native American players ever benefited."

Fueled by their underdog status, by the quiet controlled fire of their coach, and by their rabid fans, the Lady Chieftains worked harder than ever in preparation for the 1987-88 season. Their style was looser, more improvisational than that of the militant Broncos. You might call the Shiprock style Jerry-ball. It even featured Harlem Globetrotter-like warm-up drills designed to intimidate the opposing team.

"Jerry had ways to motivate you," Lee said. "You didn't want to disappoint him, but not out of fear of discipline. You wanted to show him you had the ability, the talent, the heart. You didn't want to fail in front of him. Somehow, he'd get you to do things you never thought you could do."

While Richardson got his team ready, expectations grew in the town of Shiprock which, with its high rates of unemployment and poverty, was a place always in need of good news. Basketball has long been a favorite pastime on the Navajo reservation, and the game could be a rallying point. (The savvy President Clinton, visiting the Navajo reservation in 2000, brought along superstar player Rebecca Lobo; she sat next to Jesse Jackson on the podium.) As they began to win, the Lady Chieftains became a source of pride on the reservation, a homegrown team with style, confidence, and passion. At the end of the 1987-88 regular season, the Chieftains were 20-1, including two wins over their rivals, the Lady Broncos. They seemed as unbeatable as Kirtland once had. "What do you get when you cross a Thunderbird with a Chieftain?" a sportswriter for Farmington's *Daily Times* asked, after Shiprock beat Zuni 96-33. "A mutilated Thunderbird!"

The devoted fans followed every shot. At times it seemed like the entire town was driving from game to game, their cars decorated with the names of their favorite players. Kirtland beat Shiprock in a close game in the district championship, but both teams emerged head to head once again at the state tournament. On March 5, 1988, in the state championship game, the Broncos and Chieftains met in Albuquerque in front of more than 8,000 spectators, then the largest crowd to ever see a girls' high school event in New Mexico. The score bounced back and forth. Shiprock was down thirteen points in the third quarter, but the tenacious Lady Chiefs clawed back, playing swarming defense, harassing the Broncos' ball handlers and finally hitting their open shots.

It was a wild final minute. Natasha Johnson blocked one of the Broncos' shots with forty-three seconds left, and Vernetta Begay tied the game with a basket soon after. And, as perhaps the basketball gods had decreed, these two rivals, who had played two overtime games the year before, were deadlocked at the end of regulation play. The tension on the court was thick. This time, Shiprock scored first and held on. The final score was 60-58.

Though some might say the 1988 championship was just the beginning of the Lady Chieftains' story — Shiprock would win the next two titles — this victory remains the sweetest, for the fans and for the players. Jerry's kids demonstrated that "this group of little Native girls," as Lee described her team, could beat the big bad Broncos. The ecstatic town held an enormous celebration for their new heroes. "The community of Shiprock finally had the feeling of being successful at something," said Lee. "With all of the racial tensions, and us being the underdogs, it was David versus Goliath. That's what it felt like."

Others have appreciated the drama of the Kirtland-Shiprock rivalry. Derby, who spent about ten years following the team, completed his impressive documentary about Richardson and the Lady Chiefs, entitled *Rocks with Wings*, in 2001. Three years later, Chris Eyre, the director of *Smoke Signals*, created *Edge of America*, a feature film about the miracle in Shiprock. It was the opening-night film at the 2004 Sundance Film Festival.

Though proud of their championship trophy, Lee and her teammates acknowledge that their biggest victory was developing a sense of pride and confidence off the court. Richardson's success in sending his players off to college was remarkable: nearly every one of his players over an eight-year span went on to higher education, a few to play ball, others on academic scholarship. "You hear about other successful athletic programs in Native communities, but they didn't necessarily sustain the athletes beyond the court," Derby said. "Not only was the Shiprock team helpful in encouraging pride in the community, but Jerry was really helping build three-dimensional human beings."

Lee, who has six younger sisters, said she and her teammates became role models for kids desperately in need of them. "When I grew up, it wasn't in us to go outside of the reservation," said Lee, who today works for a computer company in Pasadena, California. "Every once in a while, you'd hear 'Oh, so-and-so is living in New York City,' and everyone would say, 'Wow!' But it wasn't common. Jerry gave us the chance to better ourselves and really believe in our abilities."

Richardson, too, moved on to bigger things. It took him only three years to transform the floundering University of Southern Florida Bulls into a nationally ranked team. But on August 31, 1996, a driver in a stolen car ran head-on into Richardson's vehicle, killing the forty-year-old coach.

The players still miss Richardson and, more than five years after his death, his aura seems to fill the Chieftain Pit, Shiprock High's gym. "Whenever I go home, I'm reminded that he's not with us anymore," Lee said. "But most of the time, I think he is still there. And for me, he still is."

Richardson may have been smiling down on the Chieftain Pit as recently as March 2002: his girls had their best season since he left Shiprock, beating Portales 75-60 for the state championship. Richardson's players retain their celebrity around the reservation. Lee said she's still occasionally asked for her autograph. In his short story "The Only Traffic Signal on the Reservation Doesn't Flash Red Anymore," Sherman Alexie writes about a basketball player who became a legend after flying from one end of the court to the other and dunking the ball for the only basket of his career.

"A reservation hero is remembered," Alexie wrote. "A reservation hero is a hero forever. In fact, their status grows over the years as the stories are told and retold."

OUR OWN HOMER
The New World's First Epic Poem

In January 1598, Don Juan de Oñate set off from Mexico to begin colonizing the land known as *nueva Mexico*. He brought with him 400 men, 83 wagons, 7,000 head of cattle . . . and one poet. That was Gaspar Peréz de Villagrá, who made note of all of the fantastic and horrible events of Oñate's historic expedition and later published *Historia de la Nueva Mexico,* an epic poem in thirty-four cantos. While literary scholars might debate the aesthetic value of the poem, *Historia* nonetheless is a remarkable text, both a vision of the collision between two worlds and a detailed portrait of New Mexico before colonization.

Educated at Salamanca, Spain's finest university, Villagrá was an enthusiastic writer, one who perhaps envisioned himself the Virgil of the New World. Familiar with the conventions of epic poetry and attuned to the details of a new land, Villagrá seemed to have a deep appreciation of New Mexico. Here he writes about northern New Mexico:

> It was abundant in metals,
> With beauteous pastures, mountains, springs, rivers
> And glens, meadows, small camps, and plains
> Where they had come upon a quantity
> Of the wild chickens of the land,
> Lizards and Spanish partridges,
> And pearl-shells, for they had been near
> That land of pearls which mighty God

Has wished to be kept in silence,
He knows for why and he tells not,
And many people, all of them friendly,
Extremely beautiful.
  — Canto XVIII, lines 400–411

Villagrá may not have been successful in his attempt to write the *Aenied* of the New World, or to project Oñate as a mythic hero on the level of Aeneas, but *Historia* remains one of the more revealing documents on the colonization of North America. With its combination of recorded history and poetic invention, *Historia* does more than tell who did what when. It offers insights into the attitudes and motives of the Spanish conquistadors. Villagrá paints Oñate and his intrepid band of settlers as agents of destiny, propelled by the power and righteousness of their king and their religion as they ford a mighty river, survive an ambush, convert the indigenous people, and battle for the glory of the Spanish crown.

Perhaps most significantly, Villagrá's poem offers a firsthand look at the origin of New Mexico's defining conflict, between newcomers (in this case the Spanish colonists) and the indigenous population. It ends, notably, with a detailed report on the horrific battle at Acoma Pueblo in January 1599, perhaps the most traumatic event in New Mexico's long history. And *Historia de la Nueva Mexico* is more than a New Mexico story; it's an important piece of the puzzle of American history. To most Americans, the phrase "American colony" conjures images of the Eastern Seaboard — of Virginia or Massachusetts — but the expedition recounted in Villagrá's poem starts in 1598, nine years before John Smith settled Jamestown, Virginia.

Despite having a notable place in American history and literature, *Historia de la Nueva Mexico* has rarely been available to the general public. After its initial publication, it fell out of print until 1900, when a Mexican scholar, José Fernando Ramirez, produced a new edition. Fayette S. Curtis Jr., a young Yale graduate living in Los Alamos, took up a translation of the poem in the 1920s, but died before it was published. Finally, in 1992, the University of New Mexico Press, in conjunction with the Paso Por Aqui Series on the Nuevomexicano Literary Heritage, published a thoroughly researched version of Villagrá's epic.

"I've always thought that if Massachusetts or Virginia had an epic poem, it would be kept under glass," said Miguel Encinias, a novelist and historian who, with Alfred Rodriguez and Joseph Sanchez, edited the recent version of Villagrá's poem. "I thought it was important for the people of New Mexico to know that they had an epic poem, just as many countries do."

Historia de la Nueva Mexico begins with a paean to King Phillip, and then describes New Mexico's location in relation to Madrid, Spain; to Jerusalem; to the Atlantic Ocean (called "the Sea of the North"); the Rio Grande ("the River of the North"); and the Colorado River ("the rough Californio"). From the first, Villagrá describes the Oñate expedition in terms of its missionary value and of the number of potential converts to Catholicism:

> . . . it is a shame [New Mexico] should be held
> By so great a sum of people ignorant
> About the blood of Christ, whose holiness
> It causes pain to think so many souls know not.
> —Canto I, lines 81–4

Contemporary readers might find Villagrá's complicated depiction of European-indigenous relations the most interesting element of the poem. Villagrá never doubts the superiority of Spaniards over the indigenous people, who are described alternately as barbarians or Arabs, which then was a kind of generic term used for heathens. But the portrayal of indigenous people in *Historia* is a largely sympathetic one. The Pueblo leaders are nearly as heroic, brave, and wise as the Spaniards. On several occasions Villagrá, as omnipresent narrator, imagines a complex war-or-peace discourse among Acoma's leaders.

Villagrá's poem also documents the various responses indigenous people had to the conquistadores. At times, the Spaniards were treated as welcome guests. Villagrá describes the arrival at Zuni Pueblo and in the Hopi territories:

. . . we discovered
A great troop of Indians who came with
A quantity of meal which they sprinkled
With great rapidity on all our folk. . . .
They brought, with the height of rejoicing
All sorts of things to eat in abundance.
   —Canto XVIII, 314–325

But there was resistance, too. At Acoma, the tensions between Oñate's men and the tribe had reached dangerous levels. After Juan de Zaldivar, Oñate's nephew and one of the leaders of the expedition, was killed in a skirmish, Oñate unleashed a brutal attack on Acoma, which Villagrá described in language reminiscent of Homer's *Iliad*, filled with gore and violence:

He brought his iron-pointed lance
With such a violent force and heavy thrust
It broke the bile in his body
Smashing his ribs into pieces.
And hardly had the poor man fallen to the earth
When from the topmost of a house
From on its parapet, a mighty rock
Was by a weak old woman thrust
This fell straight down in such a way
As smashed his head into pieces. . . .
His hidden brains now scattered wide. . . .
   —Canto XXII, lines 289–301

Oñate ultimately burned the pueblo to the ground ("the fire kept sending up / A ruddy vapor, bit by bit / Attacking all the sad houses") and set down awful punishments for the Acoma men. Those under twenty-five were sentenced to twenty years of servitude. Those between twenty-five and sixty had one foot cut off. Those who survived that punishment were sentenced to twenty years of servitude. The Pueblo people have not forgotten Oñate's harsh retribution.

Villagrá did not stay in New Mexico long enough to see thriving Spanish colonies. Sent back to Mexico by Oñate to round up more troops and supplies, he was relieved of his post by an official hostile to Oñate. Villagrá then deserted. It was while in hiding, Encinias suspects, that Villagrá finished his poem. Even before he was done, Villagrá, envisioning a blockbuster success, planned a sequel. In Canto XX of *Historia*, he writes of the "risky feats" and "valorous Spaniards" that he planned on describing, "if God permits me / To see the Second Part put into print."

That sequel was never finished, and, perhaps more disappointing for Villagrá, Oñate never became mythologized as a hero of the New World. Banished from New Mexico just ten years after he arrived, he is today forgotten. His name did surface in 1998, during celebrations of the 400th anniversary of Spanish rule. Soon after a statue of Oñate was unveiled at a cultural center in Española, a group of Native American activists, under stealth of night, sawed off the statue's foot. "We see no glory in celebrating Oñate's fourth centennial," a note from the group read, which came accompanied by a snapshot of the foot, "and we do not want our faces rubbed in it."

TRAILERBLAZER
How Artist Eva Mirabal Broke the Mold

In Nicolai Fechin's painting *Pietro* (c. 1928), a handsome Taos Pueblo man, wearing feathers in his hair, sits solemnly and quietly. But, strangely, bright flashes of colors radiate from him. He's not just a man—he's a mystical, exotic force. *Pietro* suggests an American West populated by magical cultures, a concept alluring enough that, even today, the painting is used to promote Taos as a tourist destination.

Back in the 1920s, however, the image may have seemed bewildering to a certain eight-year-old Taos Pueblo girl. "Is that really my father?" the young Eva Mirabal might have asked herself. She had never seen her dad, Beaded Shirt, known as Pedro to the Anglos (or Pietro, perhaps, to a Russian émigré), looking as he did in Fechin's expressionist portrait. And perhaps she felt it was a less-than-honest account of life on Taos Pueblo.

Maybe it was then that Mirabal began feeling compelled to paint a different Taos from the fantastical one rendered by visiting Anglos. And that's what she did during the next forty years. Mirabal, one of the Southwest's finest forgotten artists, created works that depicted the quiet and earthy beauty of Taos Pueblo. She painted the Pueblo's people, the land, and the culture, and in so doing, Mirabal and her contemporaries helped remind the art world that the most honest way to depict Native America is to have Native Americans do it.

Born on Taos Pueblo in 1920, Mirabal was called Eah Ha Wa, or Fast Growing Corn. Mirabal was the first of two daughters (her sister Tonita Lucero continues to live on Taos Pueblo) and grew up in a village populated by well-traveled artists from Europe and other parts of the United States. Her parents, aunts, and uncles posed for artists, including Fechin and Josef Imhoff, and also helped build artists' studios. Beaded Shirt was especially well known. Outside Mabel Dodge Luhan's house, a wooden bust bearing his image was perched above a road leading to the Pueblo.

Even as a girl Mirabal may have recognized that, with a few brushstrokes, an artist has the power to change the way people see the world. Perhaps that was especially true in Taos. The village had been established as an artist's colony in 1898 with the arrival of painters Bert Phillips and Ernest Blumenschein, and the artists who followed them out—establishing a collective known as the Taos Society of Artists in 1915—shared a curiosity about Native culture.

Painting Native ceremonial life, these artists discovered, could be profitable. The Santa Fe Railroad, eager to promote tourism, bought and exhibited many Western works, and seemed especially fond of ones depicting the supposed magic and pageantry of Native American life.

"[The railroad] wanted pictures that they could use for posters, for marketing: 'Come visit the West and see the Indians,'" said Patricia Janis Broder, author of *Taos: A Painter's Dream* and *Earth Songs, Moon Dreams: Paintings by American Indian Women*. "Many of the early artists were hired by the railroad to make pictures that would bring Easterners west. . . . [So these] artists tended to focus on the wonders of Indian life, the 'Isn't this exotic, let's go see it' elements."

Mirabal, however, had no interest in portraying her family in any outlandish way. She instead began exploring the poetry of the everyday. As others in her tribe had done, she discovered the beauty in tradition and nature. "My tribe produces very delicate works of silver," she said in a 1946 interview on the Southern Illinois Normal University radio station. "Many very fine products are produced by the method of weaving. They also make Indian necklaces and bracelets from beads . . . In addition, they make very beautiful pottery. As you can see, I was surrounded by various phases of art in my everyday life while I was a youth."

Mirabal's son, the painter Jonathan Warm Day, told me that his mother was probably adventurous and a bit headstrong. As a teenager, she convinced her parents to allow her to travel to Tennessee to become a camp counselor, and she also was able to talk them into letting her continue her studies at the Santa Fe Indian School (Taos Pueblo's formal educational system ended at middle school).

By the mid-1930s, the Indian School had begun to discard the assimilationist "kill-the-Indian, save-the-man" policies that had dominated the boarding-school system for decades. Teachers were experimenting with more liberal forms of education. Dorothy Dunn set up the studio at the Santa Fe Indian School, a program that trained aspiring painters and, over time, became known as a launching pad for Native artists. Pablita Velarde, Pop Chalee, Gerald Nailor, Joe Herrera, and Harrison Begay were among those who studied with Dunn.

Dunn insisted that Indian artists could be elevated to the status of their European counterparts, but allowed her students to work only within strict parameters. Paintings from Dunn's studio all reflected the simplicity of petroglyphs and traditional pottery, with ceremonial and traditional scenes unfolding against plain backgrounds. Some students, the great sculptor Allan Houser among them, later rebelled against the constraints of the Dunn school of art making. Mirabal, however, thrived. Her work demonstrated an intuitive sense of perspective; her subjects — a fawn, the Taos Round Dance, the washing of wheat — had both a depth and a suggestion of fluidity and motion.

Mirabal was a favorite of her teacher's. "Eva had the ability to translate everyday events into scenes of warmth and semi-naturalistic beauty," Dunn wrote in one of her notebooks, and in 1953, Dunn included one of Mirabal's paintings in a show at the National Gallery in Washington, D.C. According to Broder, Mirabal also was a pioneer among the Dunn studio painters, incorporating a documentary-like precision in her works.

"She was probably the first to do portraits — many of her figures were actually identifiable," Broder said. "They were people she knew, and had an individuality — you can see the particular expressions on their faces. She also had terrific powers of observation. Her figures have absolutely perfect costumes for a particular ceremony or particular job, and are rendered in great detail."

While still a teenager in the late 1930s, Mirabal began attracting attention. At nineteen, in 1939, she was singled out for a Chicago gallery show. "She expresses in every drawing—in every line—a truly feminine tenderness and grace," one critic wrote in the *Chicago Union Teacher* magazine. "The clean colors, simplicity and good taste make this ageless art remarkably modern." Mirabal was the only woman included in the First National Exhibition of Indian Painting, held at the Philbrook Museum of Art in Tulsa.

In 1942, Mirabal joined the war effort, sketching an a award-winning poster—it showed an Indian chief sending smoke signals urging the purchase of war bonds—and in June 1943 enlisted in the army. After completing basic training at Fort Devens, Massachusetts, she was assigned a prestigious post as an army muralist. Her projects include a mural at Wright Patterson Air Force base in Dayton, Ohio, called *A Bridge of Wings*.

As she honed her skills as a painter and a cartoonist (her popular comic strip, *G.I. Gertie*, ran in Women's Army Corps publications), Mirabal continued to paint Pueblo scenes from memory. She was a strong, extremely articulate proponent of Indian art, understanding, at an early age, the full implications of her work. "As an Indian representative, I feel that I have a very definite obligation in explaining and illustrating our art to the American white people," she told a radio interviewer in 1946.

Mirabal returned home to Taos after the war and a job teaching at Southern Illinois Normal University. She studied art under the G.I. Bill at the Taos Valley Art School, run by painters Louis Ribak and Beatrice Mandelman. Although the school was a center for the movement that became known as the Taos Moderns, one of America's most productive modern art colonies, Mirabal continued to perfect her own Dunn Studio-style techniques, according to fellow student Ted Egri. The school closed in 1953. (Egri said an undercover FBI agent had infiltrated the school and accused Ribak of being a Communist sympathizer.)

By the mid-1950s, Mirabal's painting slowed down as she embarked upon another career: mother. Spending most of her time with her sons, Jonathan and Christopher, Mirabal's tenure as an artist was not quite through. Before she died in 1968, she painted a cheerful, colorful mural at the U.S. Veterans Medical Center in Albuquerque; it depicted wild horses at play.

Hoping to fortify his mother's important legacy, Warm Day has begun working on a biography. Egri also has done his part to sustain Mirabal's reputation as an artist, cataloging a handful of her works for Taos's Harwood Museum. Egri believes that Mirabal's work, though largely forgotten, is an important link in the chain of Southwestern art and a reminder of its deep roots.

"I was getting tired of hearing everybody say that art started in Taos with the Taos art colony," said Egri, who has lived more than fifty of his ninety-plus years in Taos. "That's nonsense—the Native American and Hispanic artists were here long before the Anglos arrived. . . . The Native people weren't just the first people here, they were the first artists here."

That's only one reason Mirabal's legacy is an important one. She entered the largely boys-only club of art making in the 1930s, and proved herself an equal. She balanced her love of country with a determined loyalty to her home, and fused a sense of the modern with a respect for the traditional. Perhaps most important, Eva Mirabal left an example for other Native painters, serving as an ambassador and advocate for those whose work had been long neglected.

"Although most people overlook the fact, American Indian art is the only true American art because it originated here," Mirabal said in the 1946 Southern Illinois Normal radio interview. "The type that most people recognize as 'American' true art is really borrowed from some foreign land."

AFTER THE ERUPTION
A Geologic History of the Valles Caldera

The volcano blew about 1.2 million years ago, spewing ash as far as 500 miles away. It welded hot rock atop hot rock, rearranging the landscape. Entire plateaus formed where there were none and debris 1,000 feet deep was dumped in places. The volcano emitted about 150 times as much material as Mount Saint Helens spewed in 1980, enough to change the weather. Its ash flows, blowing at hurricane-gale force, buried small mountains. Finally, having vented the gas-rich magma beneath its surface, the volcano collapsed onto itself. The result? The Valles Caldera, a twelve-mile-wide geological wonder most easily seen from Route 4 outside of Los Alamos.

This surprisingly pristine, open area is part of a culturally and environmentally significant portion of land. Geologists call it the perfect caldera, admiring its nearly symmetrical shape and its pristine condition. It's filled with a remarkable range of wildlife, having served as a kind of private nature preserve for years. And before that, the caldera was a special site for both the Santa Clara and Jemez Pueblo tribes, a place that, according to historian Joe Sando of Jemez Pueblo, has been essential for practical and spiritual reasons for hundreds of years.

"This land is very dear to the people," said Sando, the author of five books, including *Pueblo People: Ancient Traditions, Modern Lives.* "It was the former homeland for the people, a place for many uses, for hunting, and water, to collect flagstone for fireplaces, and to catch eagles for ceremonial purposes. And there are Jemez Pueblo ruins on the land."

Sando said he knows of no stories or folklore that would indicate that the Pueblo people knew they were living on a former volcano. In fact, the geological significance of the Valles Caldera may have become evident only with the advent of aerial photography, which showed the caldera's perfect shape.

Though easy to see from the sky or from the road, the Valles Caldera has been difficult to access for years. It's been in private hands, in one form or another, since at least the turn of the century. But as of November 2000, the land — described as the "Yellowstone of New Mexico" — became public property, purchased by the U.S. government. And now an area of land that has been of key importance to those who look to the past to better understand the present, including geologists and the Pueblo tribal members, will be protected into the future.

Research geologist Dr. Fraser Goff, formerly of the Los Alamos National Laboratory, believes Valles Caldera is a significant site due to its size and its geometric formations. It is, he adds, "the world's [best example] of a resurgent caldera." "Before satellites and airplanes it was difficult to get a visual image of Valles because of its scale," said Goff, who has been studying the caldera since 1978. "But once scientists were able to visualize how big the caldera is, it was clear that it was an important site. This is the caldera that volcanologists compare all the others to."

It doesn't hurt that the land has remained largely undeveloped, if not completely free of human activity. The great-great-grandparents of contemporary tribal members from Jemez and Santa Clara Pueblos hunted the land and called parts of it home, even after the State of New Mexico offered a big chunk of it to Luis Maria Cabeza de Baca in 1860, as compensation for land taken from him near Las Vegas, New Mexico. Some historians believe Baca took ownership of the land, but Sando said there is no evidence that he did.

In any case, what became known as the Baca Ranch or the Valle Grande changed hands numerous times during the early part of the twentieth century, until Frank Bond turned it into a cattle ranch in 1926. He allowed the land to be grazed and logged, a practice that was curtailed when James Patrick Dunigan bought it in 1960. The Dunigan family first hoped to strike oil, and failing that, to use the geothermal power beneath the surface to generate electricity. However, the Dunigans soon decided that the nearly 100,000 acres of wild meadows and mountains were most useful as natural habitat. During the past forty years the land has slowly been returning to a more wild state.

Today, 7,500 elk roam the ranch, along with bald eagles and abundant trout. It's also a scenic place, the backdrop for ads for Stetson hats and Marlboro cigarettes. And it has been a private one. Other than those who could afford to spend $10,000 for elk-hunting licenses, few were allowed to set foot on the land. Even scientists were forced to jump through legal hoops to enter the Baca Ranch. "You couldn't say you wanted to look into the rocks and just waltz in there," Goff said. "People who persevered could get inside, and a lot of good work has been done there. But far more scientists have studied the data gathered there than have actually been inside."

Thanks to a $101 million deal signed in 2002 by President Bill Clinton, the Baca Ranch, which encompasses most of the caldera, is now in the hands of the federal government. Decisions on the uses of the land will be made by a nine-member board of trustees, who have been charged with making the old Baca Ranch profitable by 2015. Access could become much simpler for scientists, as well as tourists, hunters, ranchers, loggers, hikers, and skiers. But while government ownership of the Valles Caldera protects it from being carved up by developers, some conservationists express concerns that economic necessities will outweigh environmental ones, a major worry for one of the last preserved ecosystems in northern New Mexico and the home to seventeen threatened or endangered species. After a brief grace period, the property will need to generate enough income to support itself.

Nevertheless, one group is wholeheartedly celebrating the sale. Santa Clara Pueblo, as part of the deal, was able to purchase 5,000 acres of their former homeland, including the headwaters of the Santa Clara Creek, which tribal member Alvin Warren described as essential to the tribe. After decades of failed attempts, the transfer of land was a dream come true for the Santa Clara people.

"We have been living with a sense of displacement—sometimes we've had no access to the land we've been visiting for hundreds of thousands of years," said Warren, who helped coordinate the land deal and who is now focusing on recovering other sacred areas. "These sites are of great cultural significance for us. This was an important victory, and I hope it is just the beginning."

It should be, as long as geological forces don't have intentions. An article published in the May 1995 *Geology* suggested that the caldera could erupt at any time, and without much warning. Of course, that's only happened twice in the past 1.8 million years, so no need to cancel your weekend plans.

SPOTLIGHT:
NEW MEXICO, THE VOLCANO STATE
By Dr. Larry Crumpler

With its high concentration of young, well-exposed, and un-eroded volcanoes, and one of only four or five of the world's big continental rifts, New Mexico is the perfect place to study the geology of volcanoes. Twenty percent of the U.S. National Parks and Monuments based on volcanic themes are in New Mexico, including Valles Caldera, perhaps the best example of a large young caldera in the world.

There's no other place on the continent where you can so easily access different kinds of volcanoes from metropolitan areas. From Santa Fe, Albuquerque, or Las Cruces, you can visit a volcanic feature in a matter of minutes. And the climate of New Mexico helps preserve volcanologic features. While most other volcanic areas on the continent are extensively "water damaged," New Mexico is a giant air-conditioned museum for volcanic phenomena. Even New Mexico's eroded volcanoes aren't badly weathered, with the surface features intact.

Every major type of volcanic landform, including many varieties of volcanoes, ash and lava flows, craters, and calderas, occurs in New Mexico. Kilimanjaro may be more spectacular than Mount Taylor, and Hawaii's volcanoes more active than New Mexico's, but big, hard-to-miss volcanoes aren't necessarily the best references.

The last eruption in New Mexico—several cubic kilometers of basalt at McCartys and El Malpais—occurred 3,000 years ago. And the record of volcanism in New Mexico is continuous over tens of millions of years. So volcanism in New Mexico is dormant but not "extinct."

Here are my top seven recommended places for beginning volcanologists to explore New Mexico's volcanic past . . . and imagine its future.

Capulin Volcano National Monument (thirty-three miles east of Raton) With a paved road to the summit crater, a rim trail and a trail to the bottom of the crater, this is one of the most accessible volcanoes in the country.

El Malpais National Monument and Zuni Bandera Volcanic Field (seventy-two miles west of Albuquerque) This "Hawaii in the desert Southwest" allows visitors to see how principal lava-flow structures form.

Petroglyph National Monument (Albuquerque's west side) The petroglyphs were drawn on lava flows that came from a classic fissure. This site includes both unusual small-scale volcanic features and some typical examples of the interior of lava flows.

Rio Puerco Volcanic Necks (thirty miles west of Bernalillo) This offers visitors one the world's best of the near-surface interiors of small volcanoes. And the setting is classic Southwest, with buttes and mesas.

Valles Caldera (forty miles west-northwest of Santa Fe) Quite simply, from the perspective of morphology, the Valles Caldera is a better example of a supervolcano than Yellowstone. It is the poster child for large calderas.

Valley of Fires State Recreation Area (three miles west of Carrizzo) One of the longest young lava flows in the world, with features often seen in textbook examples of young lava flows.

Zuni Salt Lake Crater (County Road 601 between Fence Lake and Quemado) This classic young volcanic crater formed explosively after hot magma encountered ground water.

Dr. Larry Crumpler is research curator in Volcanology and Space Sciences at the New Mexico Museum of Natural History and Science.

WHEN WE WON THE VOTE
The Suffrage Movement in New Mexico

By February 1920, the fight for the Nineteenth Amendment had reached critical mass. To pass this bill, which gave women the right to vote, thirty-six of the forty-eight states needed to ratify it. Thirty-one states had already done so, and twelve more had rejected the amendment or were firmly opposed to it. That left five states — the swing states — as the focus of national attention. So when Governor Octaviano A. Larrazolo convened a special session of the New Mexico's State Legislature to vote on the amendment, the rhetoric was fierce and the emotions intense. What was at stake? If New Mexico voted to ratify the so-called Susan B. Anthony Amendment, the push would continue to the last four states. If not, all was lost for the suffragists, who had worked for decades for equal rights.

The first women's rights convention was held in Seneca Falls, New York in 1948; thirty years later, a version of the so-called "Susan B. Anthony Amendment" was presented to Congress. And it took another forty for Congress to pass it. That was in June 1919. Now came what Carrie Chapman Catt called "monumental work": convincing thirty-six states to ratify the amendment. "Never was a measure so systematically opposed, never one whose program was so vehemently disputed inch by inch," said Catt, president of the National American Woman Suffrage Association (and, later, the founder of the League of Women Voters). The opposition spent endless energy convincing lawmakers that the nation would crumble once women gained the vote, but the suffragists had good reason to be hopeful. Catt's organization, along with the Congressional Union for Woman's

Suffrage, had persuaded the Republican Party to make women's suffrage a centerpiece of its 1918 platform. A significant number of Republican legislators at the state level had jumped on board.

But in New Mexico, on the eve of the special legislative session, many Republicans continued to waver. The leaders of New Mexico's suffragist movement, including Ada Morley and Adelina Otero-Warren, were preparing for a fight. For ten years, they had watched promising suffrage bills come before the state legislature. A 1910 bill was severely watered down (women were allowed to vote only in school board elections) and a 1919 bill was killed completely, despite a visit to New Mexico from Catt.

Unlike their Western counterparts, who were leaders in the equal rights movement, New Mexico's women hadn't joined national groups and were late to build local ones. "By 1910, [the National American Woman Suffrage Association] had two women listed on its subscription list for New Mexico," historian Joan Jensen writes in *New Mexico Women: Intercultural Perspectives*. "One name had 'dead' scribbled after it; the other woman was in a Silver City sanitarium. Hardly the base for an active women's movement."

The suffragists of New Mexico knew they had some catching up to do, at least compared to their Western neighbors, all of whom had given women the vote by 1914 and ratified the Nineteenth Amendment by 1919. "We women have been meek too long," activist Doris Stevens told *The New Mexican* in 1916. "It is time to be impatient." By 1920, New Mexico's suffragists had built a loosely affiliated coalition of women's clubs around the state. Jensen described these clubs as "political pressure groups," and quoted one woman as saying the clubs helped fuel "a tidal wave of sentiment."

Morley, a tireless writer, sent letter after letter to state congressmen, U.S. senators, and fellow women's suffragists. "Disfranchisement is a disgrace," wrote the Socorro County resident in 1916. And Otero-Warren proved her abilities, defeating a male challenger for the position of superintendent of the Santa Fe schools in 1918 and becoming one of the first women in New Mexico to win an election.

When the 1920 special legislative session began in Santa Fe, it was clear that the state Senate would pass the bill (they did, by a vote of seventeen to five), and both anti-suffragists and pro-suffragists heavily lobbied the members of the state House of Representatives. The rhetoric of the anti-suffragists included a number of outrageous arguments: voting was tiring and women weren't physically strong enough; the suffragist leaders were "hysterics" whose behavior might contaminate the entire U.S. female population; and if women were to vote, men would lose their manliness.

On the eve of the vote to ratify, it appeared several Republican congressmen were ready to renege on their promise to support the Nineteenth Amendment. Their waffling did not go unnoticed in the local press. "Suffrage Totters on Edge of Defeat by Pledge-Breakers," read one headline of *The New Mexican* on February 17. "Break Our Word to the Women of New Mexico—And Make the State a Laughing-Stock!" read another. And in an editorial: "If you turn down ratification you are not only violating a solemn pledge, making a political bonehead play and courting political ruin, but you are slapping in the face the splendid women of New Mexico and telling the world you don't think they're fit to have the ballot—or else you're afraid to let them have it."

By February 18, the prospects for ratification of the Nineteenth Amendment looked grim. *The New Mexican* sent a warning to legislators: "[We] will be a howling joke in the nation if the Republican party in this state deliberately violates its pledge and the Susan B. Anthony amendment is not ratified." That's when Otero-Warren stepped in, becoming the first woman to address a New Mexico political caucus. For three hours, she instructed Republican lawmakers of the merits of the Nineteenth Amendment. The next day, thanks in part to Otero-Warren's persuasion, most Republicans and a number of Democrats had agreed to join the suffragists.

"Ladies, It Looks as if the Worst Were About Over," read a headline in the special edition of *The New Mexican* on February 18. "Prospects for Ratification for Women's Suffrage Amendment Brighter Today. . . . Democrats Join with Republicans." By the following day, February 19, 1920, the vote had become a landslide, with thirty-six voting to ratify and only ten voting against. New Mexico became the thirty-second state to ratify the Nineteenth Amendment. Oklahoma, West Virginia, and Washington soon followed, and the battle moved to Tennessee, where the rhetoric reached a new level of intensity. Anti-suffragists called their opponents Bolsheviks and warned that the nation would collapse if African-American women gained the vote. But on August 18, 1920, Harry Burn, a twenty-four-year old member of Tennessee's House of Representatives, gave in to a plea from his mother, changing a 48 to 48 tie into a 49 to 47 victory for women. (Angry anti-suffragists chased Burn out a third-floor window; he climbed from a ledge and hid in the attic.)

On August 26, a simple but precious line of text was added to the United States Constitution: "The right of citizens of the United States to vote shall not be denied or abridged by the United States or by any State on account of sex." After seventy-two years of activism — and 144 years after our Founding Fathers signed the Declaration of Independence — women across the country cast their first ballots in a presidential election in November 1920.

At least that's how it was supposed to work. While passage of the Nineteenth Amendment was triumphant moment in the history of civil rights, only the naïve would think it ended the battle for a gender-blind legal system. In many states, women continued to be treated as second-class citizens. Literacy tests, scare tactics and poll taxes — which, incredibly, were affirmed by the Supreme Court in 1937 — deprived many women of the vote.

In New Mexico, Native American women and men weren't considered U.S. citizens until 1924 and for a quarter of a century after that remained ineligible to vote, on the premise that they didn't pay the proper amount of taxes. It wasn't until 1948, after a series of legislative shenanigans, that federal law ruled on the side of Native people. In 1961, a commission established by John F. Kennedy discovered scores of legal inequities for women. The Voting Rights Act of 1965 further leveled the playing field. Still, women were barred from jury duty in many states until the 1970s (an inequity finally deemed unconstitutional in 1994). So while Catt surely felt a sense of triumph in August 1920 after winning the battle over the 19th Amendment, she understood the fight must continue. "Now that it is all over, the spirit of 'ceaselessness' is probably the sensation uppermost with us all," she said. "And perhaps it is just as well that it should be. For women cannot stop."

IGOR, AT YOUR SERVICE
Stravinsky Launches the Santa Fe Opera

Those who build outdoor theaters dare the elements. In this case, it was Santa Fe's summer winds that were the nuisance. One of the flats on the stage of the brand-new Santa Fe Opera (SFO) was beginning to wobble noticeably, and John Crosby, the SFO's founder and director (and, in 1957, that first year, janitor, handyman, and everything else) hustled over to repair it. Kneeling with a hammer, Crosby knocked in the first nail and felt a hand reaching down to offer him another. Looking up, he saw an unexpected helper: Igor Stravinsky, perhaps the greatest composer of the twentieth century.

Stravinsky, of course, wasn't in town to play carpenter's apprentice. His opera *The Rake's Progress* was to be performed at the Santa Fe Opera's first season, and he had arrived to oversee the production. Even without his handyman skills, Stravinsky was, to put it mildly, a major catch for a rookie opera company. This was the man who had rewritten, several times, the rules of symphonic music, a man who, on the evening of May 29, 1913, actually caused a riot with a composition. The premiere of *The Rite of Spring* at the Théâtre des Champs Élysées in Paris announced the arrival of a rebellious new genius. "He is a liberator," Erik Satie wrote in the February 1923 issue of *Vanity Fair*. "More than anyone else he has freed the musical thought of today, which was sadly in need of development." Through most of the century, Stravinsky—whose work is difficult to categorize, as he never subscribed to any particular fashion—continued to break new musical ground.

Though revered in Europe, Stravinsky in the 1950s had not attained the sort of monumental reputation in the United States that he has today, and his compositions for voice had been produced in America only rarely. Enter Crosby, a thirty-year-old music lover who audaciously believed that he could help raise opera performance in the United States to European standards. As long as he was reaching for the impossible, why not try and bring in Stravinsky, now living in Los Angeles, and his opera *The Rake's Progress*? That opera, after all, had been performed only once in the States, in an underwhelming production at the Metropolitan Opera in New York.

Crosby mentioned his ambitions to his friend Miranda Levy who, he soon found out, had met Stravinsky years earlier. In 1949, a friend of Levy's had asked her to bring the composer and his wife, Vera, to Taos to meet D. H. Lawrence's widow, Frieda. While traveling together (they ended up at a dance at Santa Domingo Pueblo), the three had become friends. Levy even called Igor "pussycat." Soon Levy was on a plane to California, bearing an invitation from Crosby and the blueprints for the opera he was building on a resort ranch north of Santa Fe. "The theater is not even built yet, and you want me to come?" Stravinsky asked. But, perhaps flattered that a group of young opera lovers appreciated his works, he agreed.

The production of *The Rake's Progress* in August 1957 was the highlight of that first season. Thanks in part to Stravinsky's participation, the SFO had, according to *Opera News*, immediately "joined the ranks of important festivals and broken all records for speed in establishing a tradition." For Crosby, Stravinsky's participation was a life-changing moment, and a triumph for his new company. "Just the fact that he was part of us — can you imagine what that meant to us? I was thirty years old, he was seventy-five," Crosby, who retired in 2001 and died in 2003, told me in 2002. "He was a towering presence, and here he was, in our midst."

Thanks to the prestige Stravinsky brought, the reputation of the Santa Fe Opera immediately started to seep eastward, toward the opera establishment. In 1958, a reporter asked Rudolf Bing, the legendary general manager of New York's Metropolitan Opera, what he thought of the new Santa Fe Opera. "Where," Bing asked, "is Santa Fe?" Within a year or two, only the most poorly informed opera insiders would dare ask, and Bing himself had agreed to serve on an SFO advisory board.

Stravinsky was obviously satisfied with the SFO and Santa Fe, returning each of the next six years. Vera Stravinsky, a painter, was exhibited at a Canyon Road gallery. The two stayed at the La Fonda and, according to writer Paul Horgan, a friend of the Stravinsky's, and, for several years, chair of the SFO's board of directors, Igor enjoyed roaming the aisles of Woolworth's, looking at the knickknacks.

At the opera, when supervising the production of one of his works, Stravinsky would sit on the benches in front of the stage, or, when the sun became unbearable, on the side of the stage, score in front of him. For the company and the audience, he became a fixture, the man who, other than Crosby himself, seemed to embody SFO's mission. "His work and his presence absolutely set the tone for the Santa Fe Opera as it evolved," Crosby said.

In 1962, in honor of Stravinsky's eightieth birthday, Crosby organized a Stravinsky festival, featuring all of the composer's operas: *Mavra, Renard, Le Rossignol, Persephone, Oedipus Rex,* and *The Rake's Progress.* The three weeks of performances were punctuated with lectures and a ceremony. The honorary committee included W.H. Auden, Isaiah Berlin, T.S. Eliot, Aldous Huxley, Pierre Monteux, and Artur Rubenstein. President John F. Kennedy wired his congratulations: "The spirit of the man is ever young and his music is still reaching out to those borderlands where genuine creation in the arts takes place."

The scope and ambition of the Stravinsky festival impressed many throughout the opera world. "[The company] made clear their answer to Rudolf Bing's question of a few years back: 'Where is Santa Fe?'" wrote critic Irvin Kolodin in the *Saturday Review.* "The answer is: 'Where they do more varied works of Stravinsky in weeks than the Metropolitan has done in decades.'" Stravinsky himself was greatly pleased, telling the *New York Herald Tribune* that "Santa Fe is my family. So the celebration is like having my birthday at home."

If the Stravinsky festival of 1962 left its mark on the opera world, what many Santa Feans remember about Stravinsky were the concerts at the cathedral. Each summer, at the Saint Francis Cathedral in downtown Santa Fe, Stravinsky conducted one of his sacred compositions. Though the American Catholic Church had never before allowed a secular organization to perform in a cathedral, Horgan in 1958 convinced Archbishop Edwin Vincent Byrne to do just that. Horgan recalls, in his book *Encounters with Stravinsky*, the conversation:

> The Archbishop mused briefly aloud.
> "Stravinsky? He is the foremost of composers today?"
> "Oh, yes, Your Excellency. It would be like having Beethoven in his own time."

Byrne, convinced in part by a precedent (Pope John XXIII, while a cardinal, had invited Stravinsky to perform at the Cathedral of San Marco in Venice), agreed to open his church to the Russian-born composer. On the evening of July 12, 1959, history was made. Overflow crowds listened inside the cathedral and out (loudspeakers were installed around the grounds). The thrilling performance became, for the next five years, an annual occasion. In 1963, Stravinsky received, at Santa Fe, an honor from the Pope.

The 1963 concert would be Stravinsky's final triumph in Santa Fe. That summer, according to Horgan, was a less than satisfying one; the Stravinskys weren't thrilled with their accommodations and Vera, by Horgan's account, overheard some of the musicians laughing behind her husband's back. Crosby disputes the version put forth by Horgan who quotes Vera as saying, "We shall never return to Santa Fe."

In any case, Igor Stravinsky remained a friend and supporter of the Santa Fe Opera. Crosby sent me copies of a few of the telegrams Stravinsky had wired to him: a note of regret, in 1966, that a nationwide airline strike would prevent travel to Santa Fe; a congratulatory note on SFO's ten-year anniversary in 1967; a request to help an Italian composer find a rental in Santa Fe. The two remained friends until Stravinsky's death in 1971.

The confluence of the two visionaries, Crosby and Stravinsky, in the late 1950s and early 1960s was part of a seismic change in American opera. When they first met, opera in this country was in many ways suffocating, with few true regional companies and an audience generally impatient with experimentation. Crosby imagined a new model, and Stravinsky, with his music, his enthusiasm, and even with some light carpentry, helped build it.

WILE E., INDEED
Chuck Jones in Santa Fe

The coyote, Mark Twain wrote in *Roughing It*, is a "sick and sorry-looking skeleton . . . a living, breathing allegory of Want. He is always hungry. He is always poor, out of luck and friendless. . . . He does not mind going a hundred miles to breakfast, and a hundred and fifty to dinner." In 1919, a seven-year-old named Charles M. Jones read Twain's description and decided the coyote was an "enchanting" creature. "He and I had so much in common," Jones wrote of the coyote years later, in his autobiography *Chuck Amuck*. "I cannot begin to express the relief I felt at finding a companion to my own unique ineptness."

Flash forward to the 1940s. Chuck Jones, now in his thirties and an animation director at Warner Brothers, has become a frequent visitor to the Southwest. He had heard coyotes howling in the mountains, seen roadrunners dashing through the desert. Jones has an idea: Why not invent his own personal coyote, one in pursuit of an unattainable bird? And so he did. Over the next forty-five years, through more than fifty seven-minute cartoons, Jones had his animated Wile E. Coyote chase the winsome Road Runner across the desert. It was a simple premise, but with Jones's seemingly bottomless supply of ingenuity, the Wile E. Coyote-Road Runner series became a monument of twentieth-century popular culture. Mark Twain would have been proud.

The series also showcased another, equally charismatic if less-heralded star — the desert Southwest. All of Wile. E.'s exploits took place against the backdrop of the unlikely spires, vertiginous cliffs, funky desert foliage, and see-a-hundred-mile views of an imaginary, and convincing, Southwestern landscape. Forget John Ford's Monument Valley. Say the word "Southwest" and most people will get a picture of the Looney Tunes desert—the one Chuck Jones invented as a (highly unproductive) hunting ground for his beloved coyote.

Jones, who died in 2002 at the age of eighty-nine, knew a little something about the region. According to his grandson Craig Kausen, Jones had become enchanted with New Mexico and Arizona by the mid-1940s. "He loved the colors of the desert. He'd contrast it to the Pacific Northwest. 'Painters there only need one color,' he used to say. 'Everything is green.'" Kausen said his grandfather first traveled to Arizona for square dances, and was sent to Santa Fe by friends who thought he'd appreciate the thriving arts scene there.

Besides Twain and the desert Southwest, Jones had other inspirations for Wile E. Coyote. One was probably his dad, a pie-in-the-sky entrepreneur. Every time Charles A. Jones undertook a new business, he'd buy reams of letterhead and engraved pencils. With the failure of each new venture—be it a geranium farm, a book on the benefits of the avocado, a vineyard—he told his son and two daughters to use up the extra letterhead and pencils. So Chuck's dad encouraged his son to be prolific, a good lesson for an animator.

Born in Spokane, Jones grew up in Los Angeles, just down the street from Charlie Chaplin's studio. Jones would often try and peek in on the Tramp, and demonstrated an early fascination with the intricacies of comedy. After dropping out of high school, Jones attended Chouinard Art Institute (which, with funding from Walt Disney, later became the California Institute of Arts, a hotbed for animators). The legendary animator Ub Iwerks then hired Jones and taught him first to wash, then to ink, and then to animate, cels, the individual pictures that comprise a cartoon. In 1935, Jones joined the low-budget Warner Brothers animation studio and in 1938 directed *The Night Watchman*, his first cartoon. He finished *Fast and Furry-ous*, Wile E. Coyote's debut, in 1949.

To cartoon connoisseurs, these Wile E. Coyote-Road Runner movies remain a pinnacle of comedic achievement, comparable to the best of

Chaplin or Buster Keaton. They are pure, unpretentious, daring, ingenious, and, as film critic Leonard Maltin pointed out in his book *Of Mice and Magic,* as carefully regulated as a haiku. "Chuck set himself an astonishing number of challenges in the Coyote and Road Runner cartoons," Maltin told me. "It was a form of comedic self-discipline—they had no dialogue, and the same setting for every cartoon. And then there are the rules: the Road Runner never leaves the road, the Coyote survives every calamity, they are always identified by their bogus Latin names, the Coyote gets all of his products from the Acme Corporation. And the Road Runner never causes the Coyote's problems—they are all self-inflicted. To do all of that and not have a series that is repetitive is amazing."

A voracious reader, Jones likely recognized the coyote's special place in Southwestern mythology; for many Native tribes, the coyote is the greatest of tricksters. In the trickster tradition, elders use stories about a wise-foolish character to help teach appropriate behaviors. Anthropologist Paul Radin in his pioneering book *The Trickster* describes these characters as coming in a variety of shapes and sizes, but always serving as "creator and destroyer, giver and negator, he who dupes others and who is always duped himself. . . . At all times he is constrained to behave as he does from impulses over which he has no control. He knows neither good nor evil yet he is responsible for both."

And, as perhaps Radin missed but Native storytellers and Chuck Jones knew, the coyote is a wildly comic figure. Always falling into his own traps, never learning from his mistakes, he is indefatigable, indestructible, a walking paradox. And he's hugely entertaining. Picture this: a raggedy, bony coyote straps a refrigerator onto his back, steps into a pair of rocket-powered skis, and, shooting a path of ice cubes in front of him, slaloms through the desert in pursuit of his prey. That was from the first Wile E. cartoon.

While tapping into the long history of coyote as comic foil, Jones also helped shape a new mythology of the Southwest. Hollywood and its B-movie Westerns too often painted New Mexico and the West as a barren backdrop, a rather simplistic place where the white hats battled the black. Jones's Southwest, on the other hand, felt vibrant, full of color, nuance, and personality.

"The series' desertscapes conveyed a strong sense of depth and distance through mostly realistic details; boulders and buttes had real heft," wrote *New York Times* critic Steve Schneider in his book *That's All Folks!*

> [The] backgrounds envisioned deserts of pastel yellows, lavenders, oranges, and pinks, conveying sun and sultriness without heaviness. Similarly, the impossible rock formations that [layout artist Maurice] Noble constructed were both massive and airy, impressive but non-intrusive; the ways in which they seemed to defy gravity—with boulders perched atop slender spires of rock—also made the characters seem fleeter and more buoyant.

These landscapes, said Leonard Maltin, are another important distinguishing characteristic of the Coyote-Road Runner series. "So many cartoons take place in back yards. . . . The Road Runner cartoons stand out right away because of their setting," Maltin said. "It is fair to say the landscape plays an enormous role in the series, and I can't think of other cartoon series where that is true."

Jones's love of the Southwest and, in particular, of Santa Fe never failed. The West popped up numerous times in his cartoons, including his Marvin Martian series, inspired in part by the Roswell Incident (in which an unidentified flying object was said to crash in the New Mexico desert). According to Sharla Throckmorton-McDowell, gallery director at the Chuck Jones Studio Gallery in Santa Fe, Jones considered retiring to the City Different. Of course, the always active Jones never did retire, remaining remarkably productive. During the course of his nearly seventy years as an animator, he directed 300 films and won numerous awards, including three Oscars. Richard Corliss, film critic for *Time* magazine, called Jones "the Einstein of modern comedy"; others have compared the animator to Picasso—an artist with the vision to re-imagine an artform and the skill to re-craft it. In 1995, 1,000 animators and film historians rated the top cartoons of all time. Out of the top five, Jones directed four.

The bulk of Jones's work remains vital—evidence comes with the continued popularity of his Bugs Bunny and Daffy Duck cartoons and his collaborations with Dr. Seuss (including *Horton Hears a Who* and *How the Grinch Stole Christmas*). His freshest cartoons, however, feature Wile E. Coyote, the Road Runner, and the desert Southwest. Perhaps it is their wordlessness, their pure physicality. Slapstick is, after all, the universal language. But Coyote also has proven to be a kind of modern Everyman, a character, Jones said, everyone can relate to and learn from. "We are all Daffy Ducks, Woody Allens, Chaplins, and Coyotes inside," Jones wrote in *Chuck Amuck*. "We are all haplessly and hopelessly hopeful."

SPOTLIGHT:
CHUCK'S GREATEST MOMENTS
By Leonard Maltin

I introduced Chuck Jones at many tributes, festivals and occasions that would inevitably show the same films ... but I found myself staying to watch them over and over and over again. I never got tired of them. Never.

Chuck's best films never ceased to be funny or visually compelling. And that's what's really amazing about them. I wouldn't think I could view *What's Opera, Doc?* or *One Froggy Evening* again and find something new or get something more out of them, but I always do.

Here are some of my favorite moments from just a few of my favorite Chuck Jones films, in no particular order:

1. In **Bully for Bugs** (1953), when Bugs becomes an accidental matador, he wiggles his eyebrows—and it's funny. Chuck gets a laugh just by having an animated character wiggle an eyebrow.

2. In **Rabbit Seasoning** (1952), Bugs, Daffy and Elmer run through their dialogue. Is it rabbit season or duck season? Should Elmer shoot Bugs now? Or wait till he gets home?

Daffy's conclusion: "pronoun trouble."

3. Bugs is thwarted from making music in **Long-Haired Hare** (1949) and exacts his revenge by forcing an opera singer to hold one note, endlessly, by keeping his gloved hand up in the air, just as a conductor would.

4. A poor schmo spends his life's savings trying to promote his singing frog, who just croaks in front of crowds. After he's ruined, and huddling for warmth in the park, the frog starts singing again. That's in **One Froggy Evening** (1955).

5. In an early obscure black-and-white cartoon called **Joe Glow, the Firefly** (1941), one of Chuck's early experiments with tiny or miniature characters, Joe lands on a man sleeping in his bed, and uses his light (in the form of a lantern) to explore the landscape of the guy's face.

6. I love when Sam Sheepdog and Ralph Wolf punch in, spend all day beating each other up, and then punch out for the night, in **Don't Give Up the Sheep** (1953) and all of the other sheepdog and wolf films.

Leonard Maltin is a film historian, the longtime critic of Entertainment Tonight *and author of numerous books on film, including* Of Mice and Magic *and his annual* Movie and Video Guide.

LOSER AND STILL CHAMPION
Las Vegas's Prizefight Debacle

It was to be a big event—maybe the biggest New Mexico had seen. In one corner was the heavyweight champion of the world, John "Jack" Johnson, facing off against the "Fighting Fireman," Jim Flynn of Pueblo, Colorado, on July 4, 1912. The fight was scheduled for an unlikely spot: Las Vegas, New Mexico. In the small town, the world championship boxing match had been hyped for weeks, with local papers envisioning a "fistic encounter" that would boost the economy and throw Las Vegas into the national spotlight. Though few gave Flynn (born Andrew Chiariglione) much of a chance in the ring—Johnson had beaten the Fireman five years earlier, and was now at the height of his powers—New Mexicans debated other questions the week of the fight: How many rounds until Johnson knocked Flynn out? How many fight fans would come to town? How much money would local merchants make?

Some also may even have wondered if Las Vegas would survive the boxing match. After Johnson defeated the beloved white ex-champion Jim Jeffries, in Reno in 1910, battles between blacks and whites broke out in at least nine states, with a dozen or more casualties. For many, Johnson at that moment became more than a boxer—he was the embodiment of racial strife of the era. Smart, a bit wild, and for much of his career unbeatable, Johnson was perhaps the most famous athlete in the world, and the first African American champ. When he flattened Jeffries, Johnson broke the color barrier in sports, and in a far more brazen way, more than forty years before Jackie Robinson integrated major league baseball. Even more than Robinson, Johnson became public enemy number one for America's bigots.

Many blacks and whites wondered if Johnson's superiority was a good thing for race relations. "A prize fight between a white and a black man might well carry the symbolism of racial war," wrote *Sports Illustrated* reporter Finis Farr in his 1964 book *Black Champion*.

> It was not a good thing; if the Negro lost, it could be taken by white people to mean that white superiority extended even to strength and speed of movement. . . . But when a Negro beat a white boxer, the loser's racial partisans could question the wisdom of trying to equal a black man in brute power, when he stood closer to the savage . . . than any white.

Fear of racial unrest had forced several cities to ban fights featuring Johnson (the Johnson-Jefferies fight was moved to Reno from San Francisco after the state of California got cold feet). Many worried about the effects of a public beating—especially a black man beating a white one. In fact, Johnson, in becoming boxing's most famous champion, had made his sport an outlaw one. "A short-lived attack of civic virtue had caused many cities to view with suspicion the prospect of a slaughter," wrote Agnes Morley Cleaveland in *Satan's Paradise*.

> Connoisseurs believed that the Fireman would emerge from the third or fourth round in the form of mincemeat. . . . New Mexico in that day was less squeamish about human mincemeat than some more self-righteous states, and more in need of the revenues to be expected from the process of mincemeat manufacture.

The Las Vegas fight was to take place at Jack Curley's arena, capacity 17,150. Putting on such an event was a gamble. If there was money to be made, there was also money to be lost, especially with many skittish about boxing. Local hotel owners invested in extra beds, as well as stockpiling food for what *The Santa Fe New Mexican* called "emergency lunch counters."

"Postage stamps are still selling at 2¢ each," *The New Mexican* wrote, "but otherwise prices have taken a jump."

It wasn't just businessmen who were gambling. Las Vegas's reputation as a respectable, God-fearing town was also at stake. But Las Vegas, a bit down on its luck, was willing to take the risk. Just twenty years earlier, the town had been one of the most luxurious resort destinations west of Kansas City. With the arrival of the railroad in 1879 came trainloads of wealthy socialites eager to experience the Wild West. To encourage these adventurers from the East Coast, the Atchison, Topeka and Santa Fe railroad opened resorts throughout the West. None was grander than the Montezuma Hotel, opened in 1882.

Thanks in part to the Montezuma, Las Vegas was on the map by the late 1880s as a kind of Saratoga of the West. "[Visitors] represent every part of the continent of America, and nearly every tourist from abroad who crosses the continent by the southerly route stops there for a time," wrote Clarence Pullen in *Harper's Weekly* in 1890. "Eastern men whose business takes them into the mining or cattle country like to make the place a head-quarters." In 1897, the town was brimming with confidence. The editor of the *Las Vegas Daily Optic* boasted about "the chief city of New Mexico," which combined "more natural advantages than any other place in America. . . . There is no malaria, no excessive heat or cold, no gnats, rats or mosquitoes." The town then had two daily and five weekly newspapers, three banks, a brewery, and 17,000 residents. But by the early 1900s, tourism was disappearing. Unable to pay its bills, the Montezuma closed in 1904.

By 1912, the year of the fight, Las Vegas had reverted from international destination to dusty Western crossroads. Flynn was able to rent the defunct Montezuma Hotel for his training sessions. Johnson, having hobbled all of his regular sparring partners, offered $200 to any New Mexican who could stay in the ring with him for two rounds. (None of the normally fearless local residents took him up on the offer.) Johnson's "dusky" chauffeur, according to Cleaveland, was unhappy with the fight's rural location and set about bad-mouthing the local residents, quickly developing a reputation as an intolerable guest.

Things got worse by fight night. Few gamblers wanted to bet on the sure-to-be-lopsided fight, and crowds failed to materialize. According to *The New Mexican*, only 3,000 spectators bought tickets. The newspaper frowned upon the disgrace of the "Several Hundred 'Ladies'" who attended, and described how the announcer asked male audience members to remember the presence of the finer sex when shouting their comments. The fight itself was a disaster. By the end of the second round, Flynn had been badly bloodied; in the fifth, he began trying to head butt the champion. Warned repeatedly, and badly beaten, the desperate Flynn gave Johnson a brutal and illegal butt in the ninth round. Las Vegas marshal Jim Cole stepped in to stop the fight once it became obvious that the referee had no intention of disqualifying Flynn.

With that, an angry mob stormed out of the arena. Lawman Fred Lambert hid the bags of greenbacks and silver dollars and put Jack Johnson's chauffeur behind bars for his own protection. He later released him to Johnson after the crowds dispersed. "Police Stop Big Fizzle at Vegas," read the July 5 headline in *The New Mexican*. Racial undertones were slight, though *The New Mexican* described Johnson as "grinning like an ape" during the second round. Outside of New Mexico's front-page coverage, the fight escaped notice. A small article from a Chicago newspaper summed up the amount of national interest in the fight: "If there has been any betting here worth taking notice of it has not become known." Johnson, in his autobiography *In the Ring and Out*, barely mentions the fight, describing it as an easy victory and spending more time on his difficulty in finding sparring partners who could take the "grind."

Johnson's victory over Flynn was the last major one he'd have on American soil. A constant target of law enforcement, Johnson was accused of several trumped-up charges, and finally convicted of "white slavery" after being found transporting a prostitute across the Mexican border. He fled the country, successfully defending his title several times. He lost his championship in 1915, and fought in France, Spain, Argentina, Cuba, and Mexico, and, after returning to the States, in Leavenworth Prison. He died in a car crash at the age of sixty-eight, but was not forgotten. In his 1949 book *The Heavyweight Championship*, Nat Fleischer wrote:

After years devoted to the study of heavyweight fighters, I have no hesitation in naming Jack Johnson as the greatest of them all. He possessed every asset. He was big and strong and endowed with perfect coordination. He was a fine boxer, a good hitter, and a powerful counterpuncher. . . . In all-around ability, he was tops.

SPOTLIGHT:
THE MONTEZUMA RISES AGAIN

A favorite ghost story from Montezuma Castle: A century ago, a famed diva dropped dead while rehearsing and ever since has wandered the castle's long, empty halls, singing her eerie arias. For a good chunk of her afterlife, the specter had the Montezuma mostly to herself. Once one of America's most spectacular hotels, the Montezuma had descended over the course of decades into a spectacular ruin. Where the world's rich and famous once played, spiderwebs, shadowy staircases, and bat guano had taken over.

But the fabled castle, nicknamed the Phoenix after surviving several fires, is rising again. The National Historic Trust named the Montezuma to a 1997 list of America's most endangered historic places. In the years since, a movement to save the Montezuma has taken shape, led by the castle's current resident, the United World College.

The Montezuma was designed in 1885 by noted Chicago architects John Root and Daniel Burnham. Using local sandstone to make the building seem like a natural extension of the landscape, Root and Burnham sketched a 90,000-square-foot mansion with three turrets and space for a casino, an eleven-lane bowling alley, and a theater. For those traveling by train across America, a stop at the Montezuma could be a highlight. The ledger included

Ulysses S. Grant, Emperor Hirohito of Japan, Theodore Roosevelt, Rutherford B. Hayes, and Jesse James.

It might seem a surprise to find a grand hotel in such a remote area. But the Montezuma site, thanks to its hot springs, has been popular for thousands of years. Anthropologists believe indigenous tribes visited as early as 10,000 B.C., using the springs as a meeting place. The Atchison, Topeka and Santa Fe Railroad bought the Montezuma property in 1879, built a spur from Las Vegas in 1882, and soon after opened the original hotel, an elegant wooden structure featuring New Mexico's first electric lights. Those lights were the likely cause of the first Montezuma fire, in 1884; a second fire leveled the place in 1885, and Montezuma Castle, version three, opened in 1886.

The Montezuma never turned a profit. Even hiring famed caterer Fred Harvey (who had sea turtles shipped from the Pacific) didn't help. By the turn of the century, the elite discovered more spectacular playgrounds—California, the Grand Canyon—and the Montezuma became a forgotten maiden. The hotel closed in 1903 after forty years in business.

The YMCA purchased the hotel in 1903 for $1, and afterward a series of tenants—a religious film company, the town of Las Vegas, a Baptist school—tried to make a go of it. The Catholic Church turned the Montezuma into a seminary for Mexican students in 1937. "In God's Providence Montezuma was not doomed to oblivion," wrote Sister M. Lilliana in a 1947 history of the building. "God had raised it up for an even greater purpose."

The seminary lasted for thirty-five years and, according to Dave Bennett, a resident of Montezuma and the castle's caretaker, helped support the local community with goodies. "Down in the village, you could smell that fresh bread every day," he said. "I'll never forget that bakery smell. If you acted poor, the nuns would give you a loaf or two." The church took good care of the building until 1972.

At that point, vandals began raids on the place, stealing stained glass, usable chunks of wood, even a huge brass chandelier. Others squatted in the building, including an activist group called Chicanos Unidos Para Justicia and a movie company that shot a horror film called *The Evil* in 1976. By that time, the place was a graffiti-ridden wreck on its way to being condemned by New Mexico's corps of engineers. In 1982, Armand Hammer bought the property, including 110 acres of land, for $1 million, intending to set up an American branch of the United World College—a school for aspiring diplomats. That's when the building's fortunes took a turn.

In 1997, the National Trust for Historic Preservation recognized the castle as one of America's most endangered historic places. The following year, the White House Millennium Council named it an "America's Treasure," the first building west of the Mississippi so honored. That's when the fund-raising kicked in. Three years later, the United World College hosted an opening event, showcasing a $10.5 million renovation, including new housing, a dining room, a student center, and the Bartos Institute for the Constructive Engagement of Conflict. In attendance was Queen Noor of Jordan, an appearance that helped return celebrity status to a castle that, a century ago, was accustomed to hosting royalty and heads of state.

PAVING HISTORY
The Gentrification of Canyon Road

"Murder on Canyon Road! Murder!" screamed legendary Santa Fe artist Tommy Macaione at a town meeting in 1962. "I beg of you, save Canyon Road!" Macaione's outburst was inspired by what he saw as a travesty: a plan by the city of Santa Fe to pave Canyon Road. The street was then in its first stages of becoming a thriving arts colony, and Macaione worried that the charm and integrity of one of the city's oldest thoroughfares would be lost once the ruts and mud disappeared.

Resistance, of course, was futile; as progress marches forward, roads must be paved. And today, the smooth, one-way Canyon Road is one of the world's most picturesque, lined with magnificent adobe homes, galleries, and restaurants. It's one of the most visited tourist spots in Santa Fe. But many would argue that something essential was lost when the road was paved. Paving meant more traffic; more traffic meant more tourists; more tourists meant more businesses. And more businesses meant the locals, some of whom had generations-long connections to the land, were being slowly, painfully, squeezed out.

Before the arrival of Europeans, Pueblo Indians traveled the original trail up Santa Fe Canyon, making a rugged day-long hike to Pecos Pueblo. Trappers and woodsmen later used the trail to access the high country above town. Soon, there was a push to modernize the trail.

"Those who have not contributed have yet plenty of time to do the right thing," wrote *The New Mexican* on August 4, 1891, in a plea to help clear the road. "Either send your name and $1 to A. T. Grigg & Co's store, or have your hired man on-hand with a shovel." The road then was called El Camino del Cañon, and visitors sometimes moaned about its condition. John Conway, Santa Fe's superintendent of schools, complained in 1907 that the road was "almost impassable in places. . . rocks had tumbled down the mountain side, obstructing the roadway and making it dangerous for a vehicle to pass."

As families began to settle the neighborhood, it took on an agrarian quality. Acequias spidering down from the canyon allowed families to irrigate groves of fruit trees and vegetable gardens. Goats and sheep grazed in some of the yards. What is now Patrick Smith Park was then a strawberry farm. Edward Gonzales has lived all his life in the neighborhood on a piece of property passed down from his great-grandfather. He remembers bundles of wood arriving at his house. "You'd buy a donkey load. I can't remember what the cost was," he said. "The donkeys were loaded up, you'd pull a cord and the wood would come down."

The road was rough, but most residents seemed to feel it served their needs just fine. Many thought the "improvements" to Canyon Road (the name was changed in 1951) were not always for the better. Macaione and a vocal coalition of residents were successful at stalling the city's attempts to pave the road through the 1960s.

Roman Salazar, who owns several houses and the parking lot across from Camino Monte Sol, was born on Canyon Road and has lived there since. "Everybody was poor but we didn't know it—we were all equal," he said, remembering his childhood. "The area was all residential, just families. If you'd go around noontime, you'd smell the aroma of beans, chile, some posole, tortillas especially. And people used to help each other. Some people were on welfare, and the check didn't go very far after groceries. My dad had a meat market, and when someone was lacking in groceries or the head of the house was sick, he used to send us: 'Go take this to so-and-so.' Most of the stores did the same thing."

Some neighbors protected one another. Others turned Canyon Road into a sometimes-dangerous area, especially in the post-World War II era and especially after dark. Gonzales, who served on the Santa Fe City Council from 1974 to 1978, remembers the stretch of Canyon Road north of Camino Monte Sol as the poorest, roughest part of Santa Fe. "We didn't have gangs like you hear about today, but groups of kids in certain neighborhoods stuck together," he said. "You had to. It was very territorial."

Salazar remembers each area along Canyon Road having its own identity. Youngsters had allegiances to their neighborhoods, which were called, east to west, Dog Patch, Chinatown, Sleepytown, and Banana Hill. "Sure, there were a few gang fights. But nobody used knives or guns — two guys would get in a fight, fine, let 'em fight," said Salazar. He also recalled the rivalries as more mischievous than dangerous. "Every neighborhood would dam up the river — we used to have a lot of water in the river — so we'd use gunny sacks and rocks to make a swimming hole. The guys from the west would bust up our dam and break bottles in there, so people would get cut."

But that was as rough as it got, Salazar said, with a few exceptions. Salazar described a shooting at Lasaro's, a bar owned by Lasaro Vigil in the building that now houses the restaurant El Farol. Both Lasaro's and Johnny's Nightclub, located just down the street, were considered to be among the most dangerous joints in town. "I don't think you'd go in there if you were an Anglo," Gonzales said.

Salazar described Lasaro's: "There was a room in the back of the bar where they played poker for days and nights on end. No one said anything because the police chief was in there, too." But one night, a patron got into a vicious argument with Frank Serna, Lasaro's son-in-law, who pulled out his gun and killed the man. Soon after, the victim's brother walked into the bar and ordered a drink. "He was carrying a butcher knife and stabbed Frank and then pulled him over the bar," Salazar said. "He stabbed him thirty times and then pulled him out into the street."

The resultant feud, which heated up in the post-World War II years, continued into the 1950s, with at least two more shootings and two vengeance-bent men ending up in the penitentiary. By the early 1960s, however, there were signs that Canyon Road was in the midst of wholesale change. In 1962, the City Council designated Canyon Road a "residential arts and crafts district," in essence opening the doors for more galleries. Some found parts of the gentrification advantageous. Everyone seemed to like Claude's, a nightclub founded by Claude James in the old Johnny's space in 1956. James was one of the town's first "out" lesbians, a Paris-trained chef and a great hostess, according to John Pen La Farge, author of *Turn Left at the Sleeping Dog: Scripting the Santa Fe Legend.*

"Claude's was a bar where just about everyone, from artists to cowboys, could hang out and feel comfortable," La Farge said. "It was maybe the only place where homosexuals could hang out. It really became the meeting place for some of the most interesting people in Santa Fe."

Gonzales turned twenty-one the year that Claude's opened. "There were always fights at Johnny's," he said. "That was a crowd that worked hard and played hard and wouldn't take much from anybody. But once it became Claude's, there was more of a mix of people — she encouraged a different crowd, and had live entertainment and dinner. It was better than just a damn jukebox. People would dance and socialize there."

And some, according to John Gurolla, would then head to 421 Canyon, where, he said, a small brothel operated. The house, where Gurolla now lives and operates Canyon Road Flowers from, was equipped with a cozy setup in the basement. "The chest of drawers was here, the nightstand here, the bed here," he said, pointing around the room, one of two that are about 8 feet by 10 feet — the right size for an illicit coupling. "The men would walk down the driveway and come down the stairs. The lightbulb was still red when I bought the place."

Gurolla said many longtime residents confirmed that his house was at one time a whorehouse. "Everyone knows it but no one will talk about it," he said. "Some well-known people in town were hookers here." Both Gonzales and Salazar dispute that claim. "It's never been a brothel — not in my lifetime," said Gonzales, who has lived a few hundred yards from the house for his entire life. "I could name the people who owned all of those houses."

In any case, while the idea of a Canyon Road whorehouse at least seems plausible in the wilder 1940s and 1950s, today it would be about an impossibility. The place has become one of the Southwest's most prestigious addresses. Lifelong residents Gonzales and Salazar both recognize that some things have changed for the worse, others for the better.

"Tourists would never come up here," Gonzales said of Canyon Road in the 1950s. "There was nothing to see, there were no artists. A few stragglers would drive up and back. But now it's a constant procession.

During the summer it's like a carnival." He's grateful that Canyon Road has become a gathering place but admits to having some "hellacious arguments" with gallery owners. "Most of them don't care about the people who have lived here all of their lives," he said.

Salazar likes the newcomers he has met, but wishes he knew more of them better. "It's still a pretty neighborhood," said Salazar. "Only today you don't know your neighbors."

ROSWELL'S BIG PARTY
The Fiftieth Anniversary of an Unexplained Crash

"Don't be afraid," one alien tells two earthlings in the 1951 camp sci-fi classic *It Came from Outer Space*. "We don't want to hurt you. We have souls, and minds, and we are good." If the Roswell Chamber of Commerce were to paraphrase, they might say something like this: "Don't be afraid. Tourism won't hurt you, and it is good."

At least that was the case in 1997 as the sleepy southern New Mexico town geared up for the fiftieth anniversary of the famed Roswell Incident, an alleged crash of an extraterrestrial craft. For a week or so, Roswell, population 50,000, became the Graceland of New Mexico as Roswell produced the 1997 UFO Encounter Festival. Alienists, UFOlogists, journalists, and tens of thousands of tourists came to investigate, celebrate, and poke a bit of fun at the whole little-green-men concept.

By the time the festivities were done, no new investigative ground had been broken. Evidence as to what fell to Earth back in 1948 remained sketchy. And if you didn't believe in aliens when you arrived in Roswell, you probably didn't believe when you left. Still, the event was a success, boosting the economy and placing Roswell at the center of an international media blitz.

The UFO Encounter Festival included a film festival (featuring *It Came from Outer Space* and other 1950s sci-fi flicks), a UFO conference (no skeptics allowed), a crash-site rave, and a concert by the original Broadway cast of *Beatlemania*. Though the festival was a step in the general direction toward transforming Roswell into a vacation spot, Disneyland need not shudder. Roswell's July weather can hover unpleasantly in the high nineties, and the town's infrastructure proved barely able to endure the load of the festival's major events. One event planner described the scene as "total chaos." On the eve of the festival, the telephones at the Chamber of Commerce were briefly disconnected. Hotels were booked solid for more than six months in advance, forcing some tourists to make a three-hour drive from Albuquerque.

Still, the relative sophistication of the festival represented progress. "One step away from a ghost town" is how one lifelong local described Roswell in the 1970s. "Roswell has seen better days," said filmmaker and author Marc Barasch, the executive producer of *The Roswell Incident*, a documentary that was broadcast on the Discovery Channel. "It's moderately godforsaken. I would say the UFOs are definitely their golden goose."

You might even get agreement on that from Tom Jennings, who was then the mayor of Roswell. Jennings's office was filled with alien toys and UFO paraphernalia, and during the festival he remained a UFO industry booster. "If you look at the recent polls, the majority of the American population believes in ETs and UFOs," he said. "It's not freaks and fanatics."

Capitalists also believe. According to Roswell officials, UFO-related tourism injected $5 million into the town in 1996. Some Roswellians are scrambling to get a piece of the pie. One alleged witness to the 1947 crash recently revised his original testimony, insisting that the saucer actually landed on a plot of land he owned a share of. Four different sites outside Roswell are described as "authentic," and Roswell is home to three UFO museums. John Price, owner of the UFO Enigma Museum, believes little Roswell is big enough for the competition. "As long as we have individuals, we'll have different versions of the truth," he said.

The media coverage of the event could be summed up by the placement of the cameras for MSNBC, which broadcast live from Roswell during the week of the festival. Behind the anchors, in the background of many shots, viewers could spot the Ferris wheel and merry-go-round from Roswell's summer carnival. The message? UFOs are great fun.

Most of the 300 media organizations that covered the 1997 UFO Encounter Week painted a portrait of an event that was one part New Age gathering, one part pseudo-scientific conference, and one part country fair.

"I'm not here to do investigative reporting," a Fox News correspondent flatly said. "I'm just here to figure out why so many people are interested in Roswell, and who these people are." Many journalists arrived with tongue in cheek, like the *High Times* reporter who said he was seeking a definitive link between hallucinogens and UFO sightings. Others treated Roswell as a cultural event. MSNBC anchor John Gibson described Roswell as "an anthropological phenomenon more than a scientific one."

UFOlogists, of course, aren't pleased with the mainstream media's dismissive tone. Stanton Friedman often calls the UFO phenomenon a "cosmic Watergate," and best-selling abduction researcher Whitley Strieber (*Communion*) insists the media is complicit in hiding the truth. "The media feeds our most comfortable expectations," he said. "We all agree that the idea there are aliens out there, doing things to us, is a little bit scary. It's easier to take the Air Force's word that there is nothing to it."

The media's Roswell-is-good-for-a-laugh coverage underscores the general belief that nothing earth shattering (or earth invading) happened here fifty years ago. Leading UFO debunker Philip Klass (whom *Time* called the "bête noire of the Roswell community") recalls participating in a *Nightline* debate about the legitimacy of the MJ-12 papers, a series of classified memos that could prove the United States had recovered aliens. "I said to Ted Koppel, 'If you think there is even one chance in a million that these papers are authentic, take ten of the best investigative reporters you have and put them on the story,'" Klass said. "If this story is true, it is the biggest story of the last 2,000 years. Needless to say, he did not."

Still, Klass blames the media, particularly TV news-magazine shows, for spreading the UFO gospel. UFOlogists, for their part, agree that they are increasingly treated with politeness and respect. Famed researcher/author Budd Hopkins (*Intruders*), after calling the *New York Times* coverage of Roswell "despicable," described the media's recent treatment of his work as "generally neutral and fair." But the "he said, she said" debate between UFOlogists and military officials confuses reporters so much that they quickly throw in the investigative towel. "If aliens arrive, we'll be glad to have our cameras here," said Gibson. "But as my friend says, 'Buddha has the truth. We just have a cable show.'"

Those in search of the truth may have attended a sidebar event at

Encounter Week — the Roswell UFO Conference, which attempted to add a sense of scientific and intellectual legitimacy to the proceedings. One man in the audience took his turn at the microphone during a question-and-answer session to insist that aliens would become the masters of the Earth by 2012. The crowd roundly jeered him. "Don't invent a religion," researcher Ann Strieber scolded the man. "We already have too many religions." That drew cheers from the audience. Religion has become a naughty word for the real devotees of the UFO movement, which likes to describe itself in terms of "scientific perspectives," "research," and "study."

"I try to keep the spirituality separate," said conference attendee Daniel Saunders, who traveled from Phoenix for the gathering. "I like studying the science of UFOlogy." Saunders, a UFO devotee, described the conference lineup as "the most impressive" and "most scientific" of the dozen he has attended.

Still, the UFO Conference, the intellectual arm of Roswell UFO Encounter '97, at times had the fervor of a church meeting. Designed to explore the fifty years of UFO research, the conference was held in a 700-seat theater at Roswell's New Mexico Military Institute and featured twelve noted UFOlogists, including writers, former military leaders, conspiracy theorists, researchers, and Native American spiritualists.

What it didn't contain was skeptics or debate, whose lack called into question the strength of the arguments. One journalist called UFOlogy "popular science, done by people without much science background, but with a deep curiosity." Despite the conference's one-sidedness, it was difficult to *completely* pooh-pooh its content. One reason is Dr. John Mack, a Pulitzer Prize-winning writer and a professor at the Harvard Medical School. Were he studying schizophrenia or child development, Mack's word would be gold. Instead, at considerable risk to his professional reputation, Mack has applied his substantial IQ to documenting cases of alleged alien abduction.

"He's taking an enormous intellectual risk," said C.D.B. Bryan, an acclaimed journalist whose *Close Encounters of the Fourth Kind* detailed Mack's studies. "He feels very strongly that the abduction phenomenon should be looked into." Mack's credentials, often cited by UFOlogists, have helped lift the UFO movement just slightly above the crackpot plane, and both his theories and his anecdotal evidence prove to be surprisingly convincing. The anecdotal side came in the form of a tape of schoolgirls from Zimbabwe who were involved in a mass sighting; the theoretical takes a culture-specific stance, implying that the Western mind is programmed not to believe in the paranormal. UFOs, he said, are "no big deal" for most indigenous people; it's part of their spiritual belief system.

The familiar pro-UFO argument, of course, offers an escape route: only the narrow-minded or fearful *don't* believe. Mack insists that aliens actually abduct humans, and the extraterrestrial mission is one of peace and healing. In his lecture, he called alien abductions "an outreach program from the cosmos for the spiritually impaired," and insisted that "fifteen seconds with those creatures is worth fifteen years of therapy."

Bryan, a former skeptic, said the history of science is built on shocking revelations, and does not seem to believe that humans are too far advanced for a cosmological revolution. "Galileo said we revolved around the sun rather than it around us. Copernicus said we weren't in the center of the universe, and Freud said we aren't even responsible for our own thoughts and actions. Now here we are, maybe a minor experiment on the part of vastly superior beings."

Well, could be. After the UFO Encounter Festival, it's true that the truth is still out there. And though Roswellians still can't prove that UFOs exist, the fiftieth anniversary celebrations offered plenty of new evidence that the little green men are good for a little green.

GUILTY UNTIL PROVEN INNOCENT
The Execution of Louis Young

Louis Young was careful to preface his confession: "If you want me to tell you a story I can tell you one and you all write it down, but maybe some day, somebody read it and find out I didn't do it." And then he told investigators how he had murdered Eloise Kennedy.

The confession didn't come easy, for Young or for police officials. At around 9:00 p.m. on November 20, 1945, Young, a convicted burglar, had been awakened and taken from his cell at the Penitentiary of New Mexico to a room deep within the complex. There, he was interrogated for five hours, consistently denying any involvement in Kennedy's murder. At one point, Young became faint and asked to lie on the floor; later, he feared for his life when police wielded some evidence from the crime scene — a set of butcher knives — presumably to intimidate him.

It was after 2:00 a.m. when Young finally confessed. As investigators looked on, he signed a statement, which he himself couldn't read, admitting he had killed the twenty-two-year-old woman who had been described in *The Santa Fe New Mexican* as "a blonde beauty." The next day, *The New Mexican*'s lead story began, "Eloise Kennedy was killed by a berserk Negro convict wielding a butcher knife." Already, reporters had ceased to use words like "allegedly," leaving little room for doubt about Young's guilt. (The newspaper also consistently referenced Young as "the Negro," making his racial identity central to its sensationalistic coverage.)

At quick glance, Young might have seemed a likely suspect. He had been near Kennedy's downtown apartment on Santa Fe's Bower Street (which no longer exists) the day of her murder, November 19. He was working as part of the prison's work-release program, and he fit the public's profile of a criminal: illiterate, impoverished, with four different convictions (during his last crime, in which he stole $110, he threatened a woman with a hatchet). Perhaps most significantly, he was black — an outsider in a state with an African American population of less than 4 percent at the time.

Santa Feans focused their attention on the state's prison policy, which allowed convicts to provide free labor for state officials. (Governor John Joseph Dempsey had his driveway built by convicts in 1944). Raucous public hearings led to the reform of prison work-release policies and to a tough new law-and-order campaign in Santa Fe. With all of the furor, one detail was barely discussed: Did Louis Young really kill Eloise Kennedy? Or was the state of New Mexico about to send an innocent man to his death?

Eloise Kennedy's murder occurred during a traumatic, confusing time for New Mexico and the United States. With World War II having ended just three months earlier, the nightmares of the Holocaust, modern warfare, and the atomic age were in the headlines (in one 1945 story in *The Santa Fe New Mexican*, Dr. J. Robert Oppenheimer, under the headline "Bomb Now Cheap," described how mass producing A-bombs could reduce the price by 1,000 percent). The newspapers that year reflected a postwar bout of xenophobia: "Like Nazis, Jap Military Born Crooked," "Fraternizing with Nips Not So Bad."

Nationwide strikes were elevating tensions between labor unions and big business to new levels. Overseas, postwar vengeance was being meted out, with the daily execution of war criminals in Europe and Japan. And race relations in the States were entering a new era — black soldiers, having served with distinction, lobbied President Truman to overturn the military's "separate but equal" guidelines. Those policies left them as second-class citizens, even though they had risked their lives for their country.

Citizens in the still-quiet town of Santa Fe might have sensed the world outside was turning upside down. And then, a few blocks from the plaza, in the middle of the day, Eloise Kennedy, wife of a banker and mother of a newborn baby, was brutally murdered — a vicious daylight crime that included an attempted rape and eleven stab wounds. According to *The*

New Mexican, police, with information from witnesses, immediately began searching for a "sex maniac," at first thought to be a "foreign-looking man, maybe an Italian." At that time, Louis Young was questioned and quickly ruled out as a suspect. But as the hours passed, and pressure rose, the police again turned their focus to Young, who failed to request an attorney when his interrogation began. With a case built solely on circumstantial evidence, Young's fate rested on his confession.

His legal team, led by Santa Fe attorney Fletcher Catron, was suspicious of the confession; they asked for help from the NAACP and argued that his confession was illegally and involuntarily obtained under the Fourteenth Amendment, which allows due process. During Young's trial, Catron showed just how weak the prosecution's arguments were. How did Young have time to kill Kennedy within the time frame established by the police? Why was there not more blood on Young, if he had cut Eloise Kennedy's jugular vein and stabbed her ten other times? Why didn't the blood found on his clothes match her blood? Did the police intentionally or unintentionally contaminate evidence? Why didn't Kennedy's dog, known to be suspicious of strangers, bark that day? Why didn't Kennedy cry for help? Why weren't Young's fingerprints found on the murder weapon? And what about the light-colored hairs that were found in Kennedy's hand?

Despite the numerous holes in the prosecution's case, the jury took just two hours to find Young guilty. After an unsuccessful appeal, numerous petitions were sent to Governor Thomas Mabry, asking him to commute the death sentence. But at least one letter writer demanded Young's death — the sooner the better. Using racial epithets, a Mr. B. Byrd of Denver asked Mabry to immediately have "this skunk and arch fiend. . . . sit down in the hot chair."

Some sixty years later, Young's prediction — "you all write it down, but maybe some day, somebody read it and find out I didn't do it" — probably won't come true. But Fletcher Catron, grandson of the defense attorney, read the *State v. Young* file a few years ago and found it suspiciously one-sided. "I think anyone who looked at this case today would have some skepticism," he said. Steve Terrell, an investigative reporter who revisited the case in 1995 for *The New Mexican,* said he believed the police could easily have set Young up.

Today, it is not hard to view Young's conviction and execution as a product of an antiquated era, when the desire for law and order outweighed the need for a fair trial. However, Mike Davis, the president of the New Mexico NAACP and the director of Black Programs at New Mexico State University, points out that blacks still make up less than 5 percent of New Mexico's population of 1.8 million, yet account for 40 to 45 percent of the prison population. "Not only could something like [the Young execution] happen now, but it does happen now," Davis said.

Louis Young was electrocuted on Friday, June 13, 1947, one of only eight men ever executed in New Mexico. Capital punishment remains legal in the state, but no one has been put to death since 1960. Young is buried on the grounds of the Penitentiary of New Mexico in an unmarked grave.

A NEW BREED OF ROMANCE
Santa Fe's *Tao of Steve*

Duncan North's house in southeast Santa Fe isn't likely to summon visions of Mecca, or the Vatican, or even Chimayo. Except for a few mini-Stonehenge-like sculptures in the yard (targets for North's frequent Frisbee golf games), the house looks pretty much like the others in this family-friendly neighborhood. But don't be surprised if pilgrims begin making the trek to this unassuming adobe. After all, North's house is a sacred site — the birthplace of the Tao of Steve.

Haven't heard of this new religion? Maybe you haven't been watching enough movies. *The Tao of Steve* is both a way of being and the title of an independent romantic comedy — the first shot in New Mexico to reach movie theaters nationwide. After hitting theaters in 2000, *Tao* managed more than $4 million in ticket sales, impressive for an independent film. Written, filmed, and set in Santa Fe, *Tao* tells the story of a philosopher-slacker named Dex who, in between daily rounds of Frisbee golf and all-night poker sessions, manages to devise a spiritual path that has a growing number of disciples. These teachings are called the Tao of Steve (think Steve McQueen, Steve Austin, and other cool guys), and they help less attractive guys score points with the ladies.

North co-wrote the semi-autobiographical story and offered the use of his house as the film's central location. With the success, at least in relative terms, of *The Tao of Steve*, one wonders how many lonely-hearted men have arrived on North's doorstep, looking for tips on being hip.

The Tao of Steve opens with a bit of movie magic: an animated Santa Fe road sign shimmers against the wondrous landscapes of the Southwest. But even in its less fanciful moments, the City Different has a glow that Santa Feans will recognize. Writer-director Jenniphr Goodman briefly considered shooting the film in New York City, just because so many other romantic comedies had been set there. But she realized that the look and spirit of Santa Fe was central to the story.

"I've lived here since I was eleven, and it has really seeped into my soul," Goodman said. "And I think people want to see films shot from places outside of New York and Los Angeles." She described the production's approach to Santa Fe as "utilitarian," with the filmmakers attempting to capture Santa Fe's natural splendor, rather than dressing it up. "This is obviously a beautiful place, but we didn't want to announce the beauty or hit everyone over the head with it," Goodman added.

The Tao of Steve follows the romantic exploits of Dex (played by Donal Logue), a Santa Fe nursery-school teacher who, despite carrying a few extra pounds around the midsection, has remarkable success in seducing the opposite sex. His Tao of Steve strategy, legendary and seemingly infallible, does fail when he meets Syd (Jenniphr's sister and co-writer, Greer Goodman), a set designer for the Santa Fe Opera. Is Dex in love? He begins to find out after a notably unromantic hike, a case of severe heartburn, and nearly continuous Frisbee golf.

The Tao of Steve premiered to wide acclaim at the Sundance Film Festival, with New Mexico's wide-open spaces and big blue skies offering a welcome alternative to the urban settings that typify Sundance films. The movie also offers a very fresh take on the romantic comedy, thanks to North's honest and very funny story, which he helped adapt with the Goodman sisters. And Jenniphr Goodman, in her debut feature, demonstrates a mastery of guy talk and a talent for comic timing.

"One writer pointed out that men have been making films about the female mystique for years," Goodman said. "He said *The Tao of Steve* was the opposite of that—a film made by a woman about the male mystique."

At Sundance, the film won a special award (for Logue's wonderful performance), and soon after was purchased by Sony Pictures Classics, one of the film world's most respected distributors (among their other films are

Fog of War, Lone Star, and *Crouching Tiger, Hidden Dragon*). North and the Goodman sisters became celebrities overnight. "The response at Sundance was absolutely overwhelming," said Anthony Bregman, who produced *The Tao of Steve* for the New York-based company Good Machine. "Every screening was outstanding. And when Jenniphr, Greer, and Duncan walked down Main Street, they were mobbed like rock stars."

The Tao of Steve was born when Jenniphr Goodman and her husband moved into one of North's spare bedrooms. Goodman had graduated from New York University's prestigious graduate film program after making several short films, and North and her husband, having met as students at St. John's College, were longtime friends.

Goodman was impressed with North, who she described as "filled with contradictions, and the most successful womanizer I had ever met—a true serial dater." Still more fascinating to Goodman was North's ability to meld the great Eastern philosophies with American pop culture, creating a syncretic new worldview. She decided to capture Duncan's thoughts on tape, and distill his philosophies into a screenplay.

For the next two-and-a-half years, Jenniphr and Greer Goodman recorded North's musings, and began building a story around the philosophy that became known as the Tao of Steve. Many extracts from the taped sessions—Jenniphr Goodman called them "the golden nuggets of Duncan"—ended up in the film's final script.

The sisters were able to enlist the assistance of Bregman and Good Machine, which has produced indie films including *Happiness, The Ice Storm*, and *Walking and Talking*. Logue, already a rising star, agreed to play the role of Dex, with Greer Goodman, a professional actress, co-starring as his love interest. The film, it was decided, would be shot using Santa Fe crews and locations during the summer of 1999.

In addition to North's house, *The Tao of Steve* was shot at the Santa Fe Opera and in areas around the region, and it offers a warm, friendly, and familiar Santa Fe. North believes that Santa Fe itself serves as the film's soul. "We tried to capture Santa Fe's feel, that kind of waking-up-from-your-dream feel," North said. While we talked, he yanked out yucca roots from his backyard. "I think of Santa Fe as an actual character in the film."

The seemingly sudden success of *The Tao of Steve* invigorated Santa Fe's film community. If one determined group of filmmakers can do it, many are asking, why can't we? Logue is one outsider who hopes he can do more work in the Land of Enchantment—he also stars in a film called *Tortilla Heaven*, shot in and around Dixon, New Mexico. "It was so incredible to find this little pocket of great filmmaking away from New York City and L.A.," Logue said. "Santa Fe is a beautiful place with an amazing filmmaking community."

Bregman described *The Tao of Steve* shoot as his most enjoyable filmmaking experience, adding that the locals offered a level of commitment that he wouldn't expect to find in a big city. "All of the New Mexico folks took the film personally, giving it their passion," he said. "And New Mexico really is one of the attractions of the film."

The film brought new recognition to New Mexico as a site for independent filmmaking, and Alton Walpole, the founder of Mountainair Films and the co-producer of *The Tao of Steve*, knows the attention can't hurt. "The whole crew was local, and it shows we have the ability to do this kind of quality project in Santa Fe," said Walpole, a central figure in New Mexico filmmaking and editor of the films *Koyaanisqatsi* and *Powaqqatsi*, which were created by Santa Fe-based filmmaker Godfrey Reggio and scored by the legendary Philip Glass. "A lot of independent films spring up from directors and writers working in isolation, so I'm not sure the film will lead to more filmmaking here. But I can say the spirit of the crew and the process of making the film shows up on the screen."

Jenniphr Goodman knows *The Tao of Steve* is not the typical New Mexico film, and hopes it helps others realize that Santa Fe can host a whole range of contemporary stories. "Maybe the film will help others to recognize New Mexico as an untapped resource, and not just for Westerns," she said. "It was a privilege to be able to shoot a contemporary film in Santa Fe, and I think doing it here helped give the film a family flavor and a hometown vibe. I give Santa Fe two big thumbs up!"

SPOTLIGHT:
FIVE CLASSIC NEW MEXICO MOVIES (AND TWO GUILTY PLEASURES)
By Jon Bowman

THE CLASSICS

1. ***Ace in the Hole*** (1951, Gallup and Laguna Pueblo) Biting Billy Wilder melodrama about a callous reporter (Kirk Douglas) who exploits a mining accident, but changes his tune after the tragedy turns into an ugly, three-ring circus. Also known as *The Big Carnival*, the film was decades ahead of its time in underscoring the dangers of treating journalism as a crass, entertainment-driven medium.

2. ***Gas Food Lodging*** (1992, Deming) Fine-tuned character study of three women—a truck-stop waitress and her two wayward daughters—living in the fictional town of Laramie, New Mexico, a Podunk, trailer-park haven at the end of the line. Director Allison Anders develops the drama with a strong eye toward the importance of place, extracting moving performances from Brooke Adams, Ione Skye, and Fairuza Balk.

3. ***Lonely Are the Brave*** (1962, Albuquerque) Kirk Douglas has always considered this his favorite film vehicle, which says a lot, considering he also appeared in *Spartacus, The Bad and The Beautiful, 20,000 Leagues Under the Sea, Lust for Life,* and scores of other Hollywood hits. Here, he plays a grizzled maverick cowboy who mounts a one-man assault against the progress laying ruin to the unblemished Western landscape. Adapted from Edward Abbey's book *The Brave Cowboy.*

4. ***The Man from Laramie*** (1955, the Bonanza Creek Ranch and Tesuque Pueblo) An Anthony Mann Western that achieves near-Shakespearean depth. James Stewart gravitates toward the dark side as the revenge-minded hero,

whose quest to settle an old score places him at risk of becoming as cruel and inhumane as the men he is pursuing with burning intensity.

5. ***Powwow Highway*** (1989) A different kind of road movie as two Native American friends—a big bear of a man with a gentle, philosophical streak (Gary Farmer) and an angry activist (A Martinez)—head for Santa Fe in a mad dash to rectify a social injustice. In place of riding into town on painted ponies, they sally forth in a beat-up jalopy that they call "The Protector." Highly original, engrossing work directed by Jonathan Wacks, who now heads the College of Santa Fe's Moving Image Arts department.

THE GUILTY PLEASURES

1. ***Red Dawn*** (1984, near Las Vegas, New Mexico) Three years before *Dirty Dancing*, Patrick Swayze and Jennifer Grey united for the first time in this politically incorrect saga about a resilient band of Southwest teen guerrillas thwarting a Russian invasion of the United States across the Mexican border. John Milius's cautionary tale is violent and preposterous, but the agreeable young cast (which also includes Lea Thompson, Charlie Sheen, and C. Thomas Howell) is flanked by eminently watchable veterans—Ben Johnson, Harry Dean Stanton, Powers Boothe, and Ron O'Neal. Swayze later purchased a ranch in the area.

2. ***Tank Girl*** (1995, White Sands National Monument) Spotty spoof, adapted from a popular British comic book, salvaged by high-camp flair, a devil-may-care attitude, and Lori Petty's sassiness as the titular heroine. The setting: the year 2033. Sinister, frothing-at-the-mouth Malcolm McDowell has seized control of the world's dwindling water supplies. Petty leads a spirited insurrection to topple him; her allies include mutant kangaroo men.

Jon Bowman is executive director of the Santa Fe Film Festival, a longtime film writer for The Santa Fe New Mexican, *and associate publisher of* New Mexico Magazine. *He has served as editor or writer of seven books, including* 100 Years of Filmmaking in New Mexico.

ACKNOWLEDGMENTS

I'm deeply grateful to the editors, and their publications, who allowed me the time and freedom to research and write these articles. First thanks go to Wolf Schneider, the former editor of the *Santa Fean*, who encouraged me to write about New Mexico, and, with Tricia Ware, helped strengthen each article. Among the other editors who offered support: Michael Small of *HotWired*; Hollis Walker and Denise Kusel from *The Santa Fe New Mexican*; Kristina Bucher from *Southwest Art*; and independent editor Dottie Indyke. Thanks to the librarians of Santa Fe, who shared secrets that the computerized indices refuse to reveal.

Susan Von Brachel lent her considerable talents as a graphic designer; my brother Jonathan guided me through the publishing process; and my father, Mel, through the legal language of my first book contract. Jim Smith, Vicki Ahl, and Carl Condit at Sunstone Press brought their great enthusiasm to the chore of publishing this collection, and Michael Tanner and Karla Eoff have helped me seem like, and become, a better writer. I'm grateful to Kelly Clement and Kate Sibley for reading the manuscript, and to Governor Richardson and his office for providing the foreword. Joel and Alba gave brotherly love, and Beverly the motherly kind. Thanks to the many outstanding historians and journalists who showed me that writing about history could be — and should be — fun and relevant.

Most of all, thanks to Christian and Theo for the daily doses of inspiration and support.

SELECTED BIBLIOGRAPHY

The following books served as important general reference guides.

Hillerman, Tony (ed.). *The Spell of New Mexico.* Albuquerque, N.M.: University of New Mexico Press, 1976.

Horgan, Paul. *The Centuries of Santa Fe.* New York: E. P. Dutton & Co., 1965.

LaFarge, Oliver. *Santa Fe: Autobiography of a Southwestern Town.* Norman, Okla.: University of Oklahoma Press, 1959.

Pearce, T. M. *New Mexico Place Names.* Albuquerque, N.M.: University of New Mexico Press, 1965.

Simmons, Mark. *New Mexico: An Interpretive History.* Albuquerque, N.M.: University of New Mexico Press, 1988.

Writers' Program of the Work Projects Administration. *New Mexico: A Guide to the Colorful State.* St. Clair Shores, Mich.: Somerset Publishers, 1974.

Zinn, Howard. *A People's History of the United States.* New York: Perennial, 1995.

SOURCE NOTES

Source notes are organized by chapters, in the order that the citations appear, along with original publication information and author interviews. Abbreviated information is given for citations from books listed in the Selected Bibliography.

Learning New Mexico

Pretentious as it sounds: Hillerman, *The Spell of New Mexico*: vii.

A place that has to be seen: interview from *The West*, Stephen Ives, director, 1996.

The greatest experience: from *Phoenix: The Posthumous Papers of D. H. Lawrence*, excerpted in Hillerman: 30-31.

Winning It Back

Originally published in different form in *The Santa Fean*, November/December 2001.

Author interview: David Cargo.

The Blue Lake is the most mysterious: cited in R. C. Gordon-McCutchan, *The Taos Indians and the Battle for Blue Lake* (Santa Fe, N.M.: Red Crane Books, 1991): xx.

To recognize the Indian ownership: Theodore Roosevelt, from *Winning of the West, Volume 1*, cited in John Bodine, "Blue Lake: A Struggle for Indian Rights," from New Mexico State Library vertical files, publication/year unknown: 25.

We don't have beautiful structures: Gordon-McCutchan: 60.

Maybe passage of this bill: Gordon-McCutchan: 192.

Your basis is one of religion: Gordon-McCutchan: 191.

If our land is not returned: Howard Graves, "Taos Leader, 90, to Take Lake Plea to Capital," in *The Albuquerque Journal*, 14 June 1970: photocopy from New Mexico State Library vertical files.

He held the canes of Charles V: Rick Romancito, "Fighters for Blue Lake Return," in The Taos News, 26 August 1993: photocopy from New Mexico State Library vertical files.

In all of its programs: "Hearings on H.R. 471; Statement of Taos Pueblo Council," Taos Pueblo, February 1969: 6.

Other works referenced:

"The Blue Lake Area." Promotional publication, Taos Pueblo, 1969.

"The Blue Lake Controversy." In The New Mexico Review, November 1969.

Pancho Invades

Originally published in different form in *The Santa Fean*, March 2001.

Such things as cowboys firing their pistols: Bruce Bissonette, "Eyewitnesses Recall Villa Raid on Columbus," in *El Paso Times*, 13 March 1966: 2.

Our eternal enemy which will always: cited in Friedrich Katz, *The Life and Times of Pancho Villa* (Stanford, Calif.: Stanford Press, 1998): 552.

A prolonged session with Mr. John Barleycorn: I. J. Bush, *Gringo Doctor*, cited in Haldeen Brady, *Pancho Villa at Columbus* (El Paso, Tex.: Western College Press, 1965): 20.

Villa is everywhere: "Villa Is Everywhere," *The New York Times*, 16 May 1914: 2.

Other works referenced:

Scher, Zeke. "Pancho Villa Is Credited with Raiding Columbus, N.M. But Was He Really There?" In *The Denver Post*, 27 April 1980.

Not Fade Away

Originally published in different form in *The Santa Fean*, October 2001.
Author interviews: Kenneth Broad, Robert Linville.

The biggest no-talent: Ellis Amburn, *Buddy Holly: A Biography* (New York: St. Martin's Griffith, 1995): 49.

Other works referenced:

Berry, Norma Jean. "Norman Petty Recordings Put Clovis On Map." In *The Clovis News-Journal*, 20 December 1959.

The Buddy Holly Story. Steve Rash, director, 1978.

Norman, Philip. *Rave On*. New York: Simon & Schuster, 1996.

State of Intoxication
Originally published in different form in *The Santa Fean*, March 2002.

Frontier sin towns were synonymous: Lee Myers, "An Experiment in Prohibition," in *New Mexico Historical Review*, October 1965: 296.

If we are to win this war: "A Call to Arms," in *The Santa Fe New Mexican*, 6 November 1917: 2.

There were rumors that the saloon interests: "Dry Wave Sweeping Santa Fe Today," in *The Santa Fe New Mexican*, 6 November 1917: 2.

Perhaps the finest wine cellar: LaFarge, *Autobiography of a Southwestern Town*: 230.

It is estimated that there are a dozen: "A Warning," in *The Santa Fe New Mexican*, 16 August 1921: 2.

Shus' specialty was a raisin-apricot and the best bootlegger and moonshiner: Joseph Dispenza and Louise Turner, *Will S. Shuster: A Santa Fe Legend* (Santa Fe, N.M.: Museum of New Mexico Press, 1989): 51.

One of the more notable establishments: *The Santa Fe New Mexican*, 18 February 1927, cited in David McCullough, "Bone Dry? Prohibition New Mexico Style," in *New Mexico Historical Review*, January 1988: 30.

A story of hypocrisy: McCullough: 40.

Elks Give Old Timers Party: *The Santa Fe New Mexican*, 21 September 1933: 2.

Other works referenced:

Burran, James A. "Prohibition in New Mexico." In *New Mexico Historical Review*, XLVIII, 1973: 2.

Stevens, Lillian M. N. "Proclamation for National Constitutional Prohibition." Pamphlet, National Woman's Temperance Union, 1911.

Precious Images
Originally published in different form in *Santa Fe Trend*, Spring/Summer 2003
Author interviews: Gregg Albracht, Reed Callanan, Janet Russek, David Scheinbaum, Andrew Smith, Steve Yates.

Lookee! Roosters!: Ansel Adams, *Ansel Adams: Letters and Images* (Boston: Little, Brown, 1988): 39–40.

The roster of photographers: Van Deren Coke, *Photography in New Mexico* (Albuquerque, N.M.: University of New Mexico Press, 1979): ix.

Greatest scenic photographer: *Denver Times*, 21 May 1894, as cited in Beaumont Newhall and Diana Edkins, *William H. Jackson* (Fort Worth, Tex.: Morgan & Morgan, 1974): 147.

Hard enough to do in the studio: Karen Current, *Photography and the Old West*, (New York: Harry N. Abrams, 1978): 21.

Taos and Santa Fe were his Rome: cited in Coke: 24.

El Senador

Originally published in different form in *The Santa Fean*, April 2002.

We believe that all men are created equal: "Time of Testing," in *Time*, 10 July 1964: 26.

In those days, you didn't wait: "Dennis Chavez Is Grateful for American Opportunity," in *The Albuquerque Tribune*, 6 May 1959: 6.

Primarily responsible for ensuring: Roy Luhan, "Dennis Chavez and the National Agenda: 1933-1946," in *New Mexico Historical Review*, January 1999: 59.

The Senate chamber had been as peaceful: "Strictly from Dixie," in *Time*, 28 January 1946: 22.

I am an American: *Congressional Record*, Senate 1946: 407.

Did he say 'glory' or 'gory': Ibid.: 506.

Is it not true that: Ibid.: 1946: 402.

This is only the beginning: Ibid.: 1291.

Chávez was a man who recognized: "More than 8000 Pass Chavez Bier," in *The Albuquerque Journal*, 21 November 1962.

One of the greatest and most eloquent: *Congressional Record*, Senate 1963: 3326.

I should like to be remembered: cited in *Congressional Record*, Senate 1963: 3326.

Other works referenced:

El Senador. Paige Martinez, director, 2001.

Popejoy, Tom L. "Dennis Chavez." In *Historical Society of New Mexico Hall of Fame Essays*. Albuquerque, N.M.: Historical Society of New Mexico, 1963.

Truchas Forever

Originally published in different form in *The Santa Fean*, July 2001.

Author interviews: Jacqulyn Buglisi, Donlin Foreman, Ron Protas, Craig Strong.

I still cannot forget the image: Martha Graham, *Blood Memory* (New York: Washington Square Press, 1991): 43.

Louis and Martha, watching and *little one-room mud churches*: Agnes DeMille, *Martha: The Life and Work of Martha Graham* (New York: Random House, 1956): 175-77.

Took the role so completely: Graham: 177.

For Martha, the Southwest recalled: Ernestine Stodelle, *Deep Song: The Dance Story of Martha Graham* (New York: Schirmer Books, 1984): 73.

While Dark Meadow *takes introspection*: Ibid.: 140.

Baffling but beautiful: Don McDonagh, *Martha Graham* (New York: Praeger, 1973): 188.

The American Indian dances: Graham: 176.

I had only one dress: Graham: 171.

Other works referenced:

Acoccella, Joan. "The Flame." In *The New Yorker*, 19 and 26 February 2001.

The Wolf That Ate Albuquerque
Originally published in different form in *The Santa Fean*, April 2003.
Author interview: Joe Boehning.

The biggest party: Marquez, Heron, "Weather Failed to Dampen Biggest Party in City History," in *The Albuquerque Journal*, 2 April 1983: A1.

There are 17,000 of you: Jim Arnholz, "Does Anybody Know If Marshall Yarberry Liked Basketball?," in *The Albuquerque Journal*, 2 April 1983: A3.

The site of many mind-blowing: "Our Favorite Venues," in *Sports Illustrated*, 2 June 1999: 97.

Under all that howling dust: Curry Kirkpatrick, "State Had the Stuff," in *Sports Illustrated*, 11 April 1983: <http://CNNSi.com>.

My wife is pregnant: Dennis Latta, "He Doesn't Fit ACC Mold, But Valvano Is No. 1," in *The Albuquerque Journal*, 4 April 1983. C1.

What's in a Name?
Originally published in different form in *The Santa Fean*, September 2001.
Author interviews: Dr. Fred Begay, Tina Deschenie, Genevieve Jackson.

No good reason for continuing: Frank Terry, "Naming the Indians," 1890: <http://etext.lib.virginia.edu/etcbin/browse-mixed-new?id=TerName&tag=public&images=images/modeng&data=/texts/english/modeng/parsed>.

Careless trifling with the nomenclature: Ibid.

Other works referenced:

Bernays, Anne, and Justin Kaplan. *The Language of Names: What We Call Ourselves and Why it Matters.* New York: Touchstone, 1999.

Between Sacred Mountains: Navajo Stories and Lessons from the Land. Chinle, Ariz.: Rock Point Community School, 1982.

Boyce, George A. *When Navajos Had Too Many Sheep.* San Francisco: Indian Historical Press, 1974.

Dickson, Paul. *What's in a Name.* New York: Merriam-Webster, 1998.

DiLucchio, Larry. "FAQs About Life on the Navajo Nation & Among the Navajo People." *Navajocentral.org.* Chinle, Ariz., 2004: <http://navajocentral.org/faq02a.htm>.

Untitled informational pamphlet. Office of Diné/Culture Language, 1993.

Frontier Law

Originally published in different form in *The Santa Fean*, January/February 2002. The spotlight essay was adapted from Steve Terrell's "Unsolved Homicides," in *New Mexico Magazine*, February 2004.
Author interview: Sam Ballen.

A period of officially condoned: Gary L. Roberts, *Death Comes for the Chief Justice: The Slough-Rynerson Quarrel and Political Violence in New Mexico* (Boulder, Col.: University Press of Colorado, 1990): 3.

Apparently the only place where assassination: cited in Roberts: 4.

An exceptional command of abusive language: Calvin Horn, *New Mexico's Troubled Years* (Albuquerque, N.M.: Horn and Wallace, 1963): 127.

Take the Chief Justiceship and shove: Roberts: 53.

A son of a bitch and a thief: Roberts: 67.

The deceased was a gentleman: John Russell, "The Death of Chief Justice Slough," in *Santa Fe Weekly Gazette*, 31 December 1867: 1.

New Mexico was sparsely populated: W. Eugene Hollon, *Frontier Violence: Another Look* (New York: Oxford University Press, 1974): 183.

Other works referenced:

Keleher, William A. *Turmoil in New Mexico 1846-1868.* Santa Fe, N.M.: Rydal Press, 1952.

Miller, Darlis A. "William Logan Rynerson in New Mexico, 1862-1893." In *New Mexico Historical Review*, XLVIII, 1973: 2.

Hippies and Hopper

Originally published in different form in *The Santa Fean*, January/February 2001. Author interviews: Anonymous, Ron Cooper, Arsenio Cordova, Felicia Fergusson, Bill Mingenbach, John Nichols.

Do they smoke pot and raise grass: "The Hippie Problem," in *The Taos News*, 23 May 1968: 2.

Concerning the travels of two: "Filming Here Next Week," in *The Taos News*, 23 May 1968: 1.

Cautionary fable for hippies: Seth Cagin and Philip Dray, *Born to Be Wild* (Boca Raton, Fla.: Coyote, 1994): 57-58.

Hippies are thin creatures: "The Last Word," in *The Taos News*, 30 May 1968: 2.

Stop being used: Gerald Ortiz y Pino, "Violence Against the Hippies," in *The Taos News*, 22 April 1970: 4.

Never dodge the military: Juan de la Rosa, "Public Forum," in *The Taos News*, 29 May 1969: 4.

A leading candidate for the hippie: "Hippies Head for the Hills," in *Parade Magazine*, 14 December 1969, cited in Lois Palken Rudnick, *Utopian Vistas: The Mabel Dodge Luhan House and the American Counterculture* (Albuquerque, N.M.: University of New Mexico Press, 1996): 217.

The hippies didn't have much: Richard Fairfield, *Commune U.S.A.* (New York: Penguin U.S.A., 1972): 186.

I had a lot of trouble at first: James Stevenson, "Afternoons With Hopper," in *The New Yorker*, 13 November 1971: 122.

Look, I'm here: Elena Rodriguez, *Dennis Hopper: A Madness to his Method* (New York: St. Martin's Press, 1988): 103.

Combining a classic genre: Amy Taubin, "Stands by His Man," in *ArtForum*, October 2003: 42.

Other works referenced:

Darra, Brad. "Easy Rider Goes Wild in the Andes." In *Life*, 19 June 1970.

Hopkins, Henry. "Dennis Hopper's America." In *Art in America*, May/June 1971.

The Ghost in the Hall

Originally published in different form in *The Santa Fean*, March 2001. Interviews: Perry Champion, Marjorie Munden, Ed Sitzberger.

Everything is quiet in Cimarron: cited in Grant Maxwell, "Cimarron," in *New Mexico Magazine*, November 1935: 11.

Being one-half mile from Heaven: *Cimarron Citizen*, March 1908, cited in F. Stanley, *One Half Mile from Heaven or The Cimarron Story* (Raton, New Mexico, Raton Historical Society, 1949): 102.

Other works referenced:
Cleaveland, Agnes Morley. *Satan's Paradise, from Lucien Maxwell to Fred Lambert*. Boston: Houghton Mifflin, 1952.
Lamm, Gene. "Walking Tour of Old Town" and "A Brief History of the Village of Cimarron." Pamphlets. Cimarron, N.M.: Cimarron Historical Society, 1998.

The Big Weekend

Adapted from "The Biggest and the Best: Indian Market Takes Santa Fe by Storm," in *Southwest Art*, August 2004, and "The Big Show," in *Southwest Art*, August 2003.
Author interviews: Marcus Amerman, Annie Antone, Shonto Begay, Bruce Bernstein, Norma Howard, Rondina Huma, Jai Lahksman, Jamie Okuma, Robert Tenorio, Lonnie Vigil, Daryl Whitegeese, Larry Yazzie.

We call these people 'untutored . . .': "A Marvelous People," in *The Santa Fe New Mexican*, 6 September 1922, cited in LaFarge, *Autobiography of a Southwestern Town*: 273-74.

Other works referenced:
Bernstein, Bruce. "Indian Market." In *The Santa Fean*, August 1995.

The Rise of Public Art

Originally published in different form in *The Santa Fean*, August 2001.
Author interviews: Kathryn Flynn, Steve Yates.

My God, she has six: "What's Wrong With This Picture? Artist Produces Freak In Court House," in *Taos Valley News*, 1 March 1934: 1.
American art is anything: Milton Meltzer, *Violins and Shovels* (New York: Delacorte Press, 1976): 69.
Don't forget that the burro: cited in J. B. Colson, "The Art of the Human Document," in *Far from Main Street* (Santa Fe, N.M.: Museum of New Mexico Press, 1993): 4.

Other works referenced:
DellaFlora, Tony. "Project Finds Wealth of New Deal Artworks." In *The Albuquerque Journal*, 10 November 1997.

"Federal Art Project." In *New Mexico Narrative,* 20 August 1936.

Gabriel, Bertram. "WPA Murals — Fine Art from Hard Times." In *New Mexico Magazine,* November 1982.

Lux, Guillermo. "New Deal helped create New Mexico's art heritage." In *The Santa Fe New Mexican,* 30 August 1992.

Nathanson, Rick. "Anti-Depression Transfusion: WPA." In *The Albuquerque Journal,* 28 July 1991.

Hail to the Chiefs

Originally published in different form in *The Santa Fean,* June 2002.

Author interviews: Rick Derby, Cheryl Lee.

What do you get when you cross: Ken Selph, "Chieftain Girls Hammer T-Birds," in *Farmington Daily Times,* 30 January 1988.

They were used to losing: *Rocks with Wings,* Rick Derby, director, 2001.

A reservation hero is remembered: Sherman Alexie, "The Only Traffic Signal on the Reservation Doesn't Flash Red Anymore," in *Tonto and the Lone Ranger Fistfight in Heaven* (New York: Perennial, 1994): 48.

Our Own Homer

Originally published in different form in *The Santa Fean,* November/December 2002.

Author interview: Miguel Encinias.

We see no glory in celebrating: James Brooke, "Conquistador Statue Stirs Hispanic Pride and Indian Rage," in *The New York Times,* 9 February 1998: A10.

Other works referenced:

Chavez, Thomas A. "La Historia de la Nueva Mexico." In *El Palacio,* 1998.

Linthicum, Leslie. "History Unkind to Colonization Leader." In *The Albuquerque Journal,* 24 January 1998.

Rowling, Rebecca. "Native Americans Object to Celebration of Spanish Conqueror." In *The Santa Fe New Mexican,* 17 May 1998.

Villagrá, Gaspar Peréz. *La Historia de la Nueva Mexico.* Albuquerque, N.M.: University of New Mexico Press, 2004.

Trailerblazer
Originally published in different form in *The Santa Fean*, November/December 2002.
Author interviews: Patricia Janis Broder, Ted Egri, Jonathan Warm Day.

My tribe produces very delicate: interview with Eva Mirabal, *Southern Hour* radio show transcript, 1946 (from the files of Jonathan Warm Day): 4.

Eva had the ability to translate: cited in Patricia Janis Broder, *Earth Songs, Moon Dreams: Paintings by American Indian Women* (New York: St. Martins Press, 1999): 9.

She expresses in every drawing: "Wild Flowers," in *Chicago Union Teacher*, undated (from the files of Jonathan Warm Day): 3.

As an Indian representative: *Southern Hour* radio show: 9.

Although most people overlook the fact: Ibid.: 10.

Other works referenced:

Balcob, Mary N. *Nicolai Fechin*. Flagstaff, Ariz.: Northland Press, 1975.

"G.I. Gertie." In *New Mexico Magazine*, July 1944.

Lucas, Urith. "Heart and Memory Serve Artist In Creating Indian Paintings." In *The Albuquerque Tribune*, 19 November 1964.

Reilly, Nancy. *Joseph Imhof: Artist of the Pueblos*. Santa Fe, N.M.: Sunstone Press, 1998.

Unknown interviewer. Radio interview with Eva Mirabal (transcript). Patterson Air Force Base, 31 August 1943. From the files of Jonathan Warm Day.

After the Eruption
Originally published in different form in *The Santa Fean*, June 2001.
Author interviews: Fraser Goff, Joe Sando, Alvin Warren.

The caldera could erupt at any time: cited in Keith Easthouse, "Restless Calderas," in *The Santa Fe New Mexican*, 23 June 1995: C1.

Other works referenced:

Acuff, Mark. "The Biggest Bang." In *New Mexico Magazine*, May 1979.

"Baca Location Questions and Answers." Santa Fe National Forest Service. Pamphlet, undated.

Brooke, James. "U.S. Hopes to Buy Picture-Perfect Slice of the West." In *The New York Times*, 25 August 1998.

Cart, Julie. "Nature in Its Rarest Form Can Be Found at Baca Ranch." In
    Los Angeles Times, 19 May 2000.
Constable, Anne. "Bad Medicine." In *The Santa Fe Reporter*, 10
    November 1999.

When We Won the Vote

New Mexico . . . will be a howling joke: "Break Our Word to the Women of
    New Mexico—And Make the State a Laughing-Stock!," in *The Santa
    Fe New Mexican*, 17 February 1920.
By 1910, [the National American Woman Suffrage Association] had: Joan
    Jensen, "Disfranchisement Is a Disgrace," in *New Mexico Women:
    Intercultural Perspectives* (Albuquerque, N.M.: University of New
    Mexico Press, 1986): 303-4.
We women have been meek: cited in Jensen: 308.
Disfranchisement is a disgrace: cited in Jensen: 301.
Suffrage Totters on Edge of Defeat and *If you turn down ratification*:
    "Suffrage Totters on Edge of Defeat by Pledge-Breakers," in *The Santa
    Fe New Mexican*, 17 February 1920: 1
Ladies, It Looks as if the Worst: "Ladies, it Looks as if the Worst Were
    About Over," in *The Santa Fe New Mexican*, 18 February 1920: 1.

Other works referenced:
Venturini, Carol Ann. *The Fight for Indian Voting Rights in New Mexico*.
    Master's thesis. University of New Mexico, 1993.

Igor, at Your Service

Originally published in different form in *The Santa Fean*, July 2001.
Author interview: John Crosby.

He is a liberator: Erik Satie, "Igor Stravinsky," in *Vanity Fair*, February
    1923: 39.
Joined the ranks of important festivals: cited in Eleanor Scott, *The First
    Twenty Years of the Santa Fe Opera* (Santa Fe: Sunstone Press, 1976): 8.
The spirit of the man is ever young: Paul Horgan, *Encounters with
    Stravinsky* (New York: Farrar, Straus and Giroux, 1972): 213.
Where is Santa Fe: "New York Critic Finds Opera in New Mexico
    Lacking," in *The Santa Fe New Mexican*, 6 August 1962.
Santa Fe is my family: *New York Herald Tribune*, 1962: photocopy in New
    Mexico State Library files.
The Archbishop mused briefly: Horgan: 130.

Other works referenced:

Scott, Eleanor. *The First Twenty Years of the Santa Fe Opera*. Santa Fe, N.M.: Sunstone Press, 1976.

Stravinsky, Igor, and Robert Craft. *Conversations with Igor Stravinsky*. Garden City, N.Y.: Doubleday, 1959.

Wile E., Indeed

Originally published in different form in *The Santa Fean*, August 2002.

Author interviews: Craig Kausen, Leonard Maltin, Sharla Throckmorton-Mc-Dowell.

Sick and sorry-looking skeleton: cited in Chuck Jones, *Chuck Amuck* (New York: Farrar, Straus and Giroux, 1999): 34-35.

He and I had so much: Ibid.: 35.

Creator and destroyer: Paul Radin, *The Trickster: A Study in American Indian Myth* (New York: Bell Publishing Company, 1956): ix.

The series' desertscapes conveyed: Steve Schneider, *That's All Folks!: The Art of Warner Brothers Animation* (New York: Henry Holt, 1990): 228.

The Einstein of modern comedy: Richard Corliss, "That Old Feeling: Remembering Chuck Jones," in *Time*, 24 February 2002.

We are all Daffy Ducks: Jones: 39.

Other works referenced:

Lenburg, Jeff. *The Great Cartoon Directors*. New York: Da Capo Press, 1993.

Maltin, Leonard. *Of Mice and Magic*. New York: Plume Books, 1990.

Loser and Still Champion

Originally published in different form in *The Santa Fean*, October 2002.

The spotlight text was adapted from an article for *New Mexico Magazine*, February 1998.

Author interviews: Dave Bennett, Philip O. Geier.

A prize fight between a white and a black: Finis Farr, *Black Champion: The Life and Times of Jack Johnson* (New York: Charles Scribner's Sons, 1964): 28.

A short-lived attack of civic virtue: Agnes Morley Cleaveland, *Satan's Paradise, from Lucien Maxwell to Fred Lambert* (Boston: Houghton Mifflin, 1952): 176.

Postage stamps are still selling: "Las Vegas Filling Up With Fight Fans," in *The Santa Fe New Mexican*, 28 June 1912: 1.

[Visitors] represent every part: Clarence Pullen, "The Las Vegas Hot Springs," in *Harper's Weekly*, 28 June 1890: photocopy from New Mexico State Library vertical files.

More natural advantages: "This Locality," in *Las Vegas Daily Optic*, 25 May 1897: photocopy from New Mexico State Library vertical files. 1912: 1.

After years devoted to the study of heavyweight: Nat Fleischer, *The Heavyweight Champion* (New York: G. P. Putnam's Sons, 1949): 153.

In God's Providence: Sister M. Lilliana, "The American Douai," in *American Catholic Historical Society*, 1947: 11.

Other sources referenced:

"All Ready for Big Fight." In *The Santa Fe New Mexican*, 3 July 1912.

Condon, Dave. "Montezuma." In *New Mexico Magazine*, November 1942.

Johnson, Jack. *In the Ring and Out: The Autobiography of Jack Johnson*. New York: First Carol, 1992.

"Montezuma Castle: Tourism and Economic Impact Study." Albuquerque, N.M.: Seely and Associates, undated.

"The Montezuma Hotel." In *Southwest Heritage*, undated. From the vertical files at the New Mexico State Library.

Paving History

Originally published in different form in *The Santa Fean*, January/February 2003.
Author interviews: Edward Gonzales, John Gurrola, John Pen La Farge, Roman Salazar.

Murder on Canyon Road: cited in Gussie Fauntleroy, "Paving Canyon Road," in *The Santa Fe New Mexican*, 6 June 1999: F4.

Those who have not contributed: in *The Santa Fe New Mexican*, 4 Aug 1891: 2.

Almost impassable in places: Fauntleroy: F1.

Roswell's Big Party

Adapted from three articles for *HotWired* magazine (now *Wired News*): "Media Descends, Cynically, on UFO Gathering, " <http://www.wired.com/news/culture/0,1284,4974,00.html>, 6 July 1997; "Praying to the Aliens," <http://www.wired.com/news/culture/0,1284,4983,00.html>, 7 July 1997; and "Town Beckons Little Green Money Men," <http://www.wired.com/news/culture/0,1284,4957,00.html>, 4 July 1997.

Author interviews: Marc Barasch, C.D.B. Bryan, John Gibson, Budd Hopkins, Tom Jennings, Phillip Klass, Daniel Saunders, Whitley Strieber.

Guilty Until Proven Innocent
Originally published in different form in *The Santa Fean*, April 2001.
Author interviews: Fletcher Catron, Steve Terrell.

If you want me to tell you: transcripts of testimony, New Mexico District
Court, McKinley County, 18–20 February 1947: 33.
Eloise Kennedy was killed by a berserk: "Killer Confesses, Negro Convict
Admits Knifing Blonde Beauty," in *The Santa Fe New Mexican*, 23
November 1945: 1.
Foreign-looking man: "Twin Clues Spur Police in Search for Maniac
Slayer," in *The Santa Fe New Mexican*, 20 November 1945: 1.
This skunk and arch fiend: cited in Steve Terrell, "The Execution of Louis
Young," in *The Santa Fe New Mexican*, 29 October 1995: A1.

Other works referenced:
Terrell, Steve. "A Case Riddled With Questions." In *The Santa Fe New
Mexican*, 29 October 1995.
Transcripts of testimony, *State v. Young*. New Mexico Supreme Court,
51 N.M. 77, 19 March 1947.
"Young Says He Was Tricked Into Confession." In *The Santa Fe New
Mexican*, 20 February 1945.

A New Breed of Romance
Adapted from *The Zen of the Tao of Steve*, published in *The Santa Fean*, June 2000.
Author interviews: Antony Bregman, Jenniphr Goodman, Duncan North, Alton
Walpole.

Other works referenced:
Tao of Steve. Jenniphr Goodman, director. Sony Pictures Classics, 2000.

INDEX

A

Abbink, Emily, 32
Ace in the Hole, 161
Acoma Pueblo, 107, 108, 109–110
Adams, Ansel, 39, 41, 42, 45
Adams, Kenneth, 97
Albracht, Gregg, 45
Albuquerque, NM, 58–61
Alexie, Sherman, 105
Allison, Clay, 85
Amerman, Marcus, 89
Anderson, Clinton P., 20
Andrew Smith Gallery, 43, 46
Anti-Saloon League, 34–35
Antone, Annie, 87
Apodaca, A.L. "Happy", 73–74
Apodaca, Antonia, 32
Arbus, Diane, 43
Arts in New Mexico, 80, 95–100
    dance, 54–57
    literature, 85, 97–98, 106–110
    movies, 75–76, 80–82, 130–133, 134–135, 157–162
    music, 27–33, 97, 126–129
    Native American arts, 87–94, 111–115
    painting, 85, 111–115
    photography, 39–47, 97
Assimilation policy, 19, 63–66, 113
Atchison, Topeka and Santa Fe Railroad, 141
Austin, Mary, 41

B

Baca Ranch, 117–118
Bakos, Jozef, 36
Barela, Patrocio, 96–97
Basketball, 58–61, 101–105
Baumann, Gustave, 97
Beaded Shirt, 111, 112
Beasley, Hubert, 74
Begay, Fred, 64
Begay, Harrison, 113
Begay, Harrison, Jr., 88
Begay, Shonto, 91–92
Begay, Vernetta, 102
Bennett, Dave, 141
Bernal, Paul, 20–21
Bernstein, Bruce, 90–91, 92–93
Bird, Gail, 88
Bisttram, Emil, 95, 96
Blue Lake, 17–22
Blumenschein, Ernest, 112
Boehning, Joe, 59
Bond, Frank, 117
Boone, Daniel, II, 85
Bowman, Jon, 161–162
Boxing, 136–140
Boy Scouts, 84
Bregman, Anthony, 159–160
Broad, Kenneth, 30–31
Broder, Patricia Janis, 112
Brown, Richard Maxwell, 68
Bryan, C.D.B., 151

Buglisi, Jaqulyn, 57
Burke, Charles, 19
Burnham, Daniel, 140
Byrd, Wesley, 73–4
Byrne, Edwin Vincent, 129

C

Cabeza de Baca, Luis Maria, 117
Cabezon, NM, 82
Cagin, Seth, 76
Cahill, Holger, 96
Callanan, Reid, 43, 44, 45
Canyon Road, 143–147
Caponigro, Paul, 44, 46
Capulin Volcano National Monument,
    120
Cargo, David, 19–20, 21
Carlsbad, NM, 34
Carranza, Venustiano, 24–25
Cartier-Bresson, Henri, 39, 42
Cartoons, 130–135
Catron, Fletcher, 155
Catt, Carrie Chapman, 122–123, 125
Center for Contemporary Arts, The 40
Chabot, Maria, 91
Chaco Canyon, 14
Champion, Perry, 86
Chaves, José Francisco, 72–3
Chávez, Dennis, 48–52
Chuck Jones Studio Gallery, 133
Cimarron, NM, 84–87
Civil rights, 19, 22, 48–52, 122–125
Civil Rights Bill, 48–49
Civil War, 68, 69, 70, 71
Claude's, 145–6
Cleaveland, Agnes Morley, 137
Clift, William, 44, 46
Clovis, NM, 27–31
Cody, Buffalo Bill, 85
Cohen, Leonard, 76
Coke, Van Deren, 41, 42, 43, 46
College of Santa Fe, Marion Center
    for Photographic Arts, 39–40,
    43–44, 46

Columbus, NM, 23–26
Combs, Michael, 32
Communes, 75, 77–78
Conner, Bruce, 79
Conway, John, 144
Coogler, Ovida "Cricket", 73–74
Cooper, Ron, 80
Coyotes, 130, 131–2
Creeley, Robert, 77
Crickets (music group), 28–30
Crockett, Davy, 85
Crosby, John, 126–129
Crumpler, Larry, 119–121
Curley, Jack, 137
Curtis, Edward Sheriff, 41
Curtis, Fayette S., Jr., 107
Cutting, Bronson, 36, 49

D

Dark Meadow, 55–56
de la Rosa, Juan, 77
de Mille, Agnes, 54
Delano, John, 42
Derby, Rick, 102, 104
Deschenie, Tina, 64, 66–67
Diné, 33, 42, 62–67
Diné College, 65
Dispenza, Joseph, 36
Dray, Philip, 76
Dunigan, James Patrick, 117–118
Dunn, Dorothy, 113
Dylan, Bob, 29, 33, 76

E

Earp, Wyatt, 85
Easy Rider, 75–76
Eddy, Charles Bishop, 34
Eddy, NM, 34
Edge of America, 104
Education, 62–66
Egge, Ana, 32
Egri, Ted, 114, 115
El Camino del Cañon, 143
El Cortez Theater, 79

El Malpais National Monument, 120
El Penitente, 55
El Senador, 51
Encinias, Miguel, 108
Environmental movement, 18, 21
Exchange Hotel, 68, 70, 71
Eyre, Chris, 104

F
F-22 Gallery, 43
Fair Employment Practice Committee, 49–50
Fairfield, Richard, 77–78
Fall, Albert, 72
"Family, The", 78
Fechin, Nicolai, 111, 112
Federal Writers Program, 97–98
Fireballs (music group), 30
Five Star Commune, 78
Fleischer, Nat, 139–140
Flynn, Jim, 136, 138–139
Flynn, Kathryn, 96, 97, 99–100
Fonda, Peter, 76, 80–83
Foreman, Donlin, 55
Fountain, Albert J., 72
Frank, Robert, 42
Frielander, Lee, 44

G
Gandert, Miguel, 44
Garrett, Pat, 72
Gas Food Lodging, 161
Geology in New Mexico, 116–121
Georgia O'Keeffe Museum, 40
Ghosts, 85–86
Gibson, John, 150
Gilpin, Laura, 42, 43, 46
Goff, Fraser, 117, 118
Gonzales, Edward, 144–147
Goodman, Jenniphr, 158, 159–160
Gordon-McCutchan, R.C., 19
Graham, Martha, 41, 53–57
Greeves, Teri, 88
Grey, Zane, 85

Gurolla, John, 146

H
Hahn, Betty, 43, 46–7
Hailmann, W.N., 64
Haley, James, 19
Hammer, Armand, 141
Haozous, Bob, 91
Harvey, Fred, 141
Hawkins, Erick, 56
Heath, Herman H., 70
Henderson, William Penhallow, 100
Heredia, Thomas, 69–70
Herrera, Joe, 113
Hewett, Edgar Lee, 90
Hillers, J.K., 39, 41, 42
Hippies, 75–80
Hired Hand, The, 81–83
Hillerman, Tony, 14
Holliday, Doc, 85
Hollon, W. Eugene, 71
Holly, Buddy, 27–31
Hopi territories, 108–109
Hopkins, Budd, 150
Hopper, Dennis, 75–80
Horgan, Paul, 128, 129
Horn, Calvin, 69
Horst, Louis, 54
Houser, Allan, 92, 97, 113
Howard, Daniel, 94
Howard, Norma, 92, 94
Huma, Rondina, 93–94

I
Imhoff, Josef, 112
Indian boarding school system, 63–64, 113
Indian Market, 87–94

J
Jackson, Genevieve, 66
Jackson, William Henry, 39, 40–41, 42, 46
Jamestown, VA, 14

James, Jesse, 85
Jemez Pueblo, 116, 117
Jennings, Tom, 149
Jennings, Waylon, 30
Jensen, Joan, 123
Johnny's Nightclub, 145
Johnson, Gary, 37
Johnson, John "Jack", 136–140
Johnson, Lyndon Baines, 48, 51
Johnson, Natasha, 102
Johnson, Yazzie, 88
Jones, Andrieus, 49
Jones, Chuck, 130–135
Jung, Carl, 41

K
Kausen, Craig, 131
Kazin, Alfred, 95
Kennedy, Eloise, 153–155
Keppeler, Ken, 31–33
Ketchum, Blackjack, 85
Kilberg, Bobbie Greene, 21
Kirkpatrick, Curry, 60–61
Kirtland Central High School, 101,
   102, 103
Klass, Philip, 150
Kloss, Gene, 97, 99
Knee, Edward, 41
Knox, Buddy, 28

L
La Fonda Hotel, 68, 70, 71
LaFarge, John Pen, 146
LaFarge, Oliver, 36
LaGrone, Oliver, 100
Lakshman, Jai, 91
Lambert, Fred, 84, 85
Lambert, Henry, 85
Lambert Inn, 84–86
Lambert, Mary, 86
Lange, Dorothea, 42
Larrazolo, Octaviano A., 122
Las Cruces, NM, 73–74
Las Vegas Gazette, 84

Las Vegas, NM, 136–142
Lasaro's, 145
Law, Lisa, 44
Lawrence, D.H., 15, 41
Lee, Cheryl, 102–105
Lee, Russell, 42
Lennon, John, 27, 29
Levy, Miranda, 127
Lilliana, Sister M., 141
Linville, Robert, 29–31
Logue, Donal, 158
Lonely Are the Brave, 161
Los Chaves, NM, 49
Luhan, Mabel Dodge, 17, 41, 76, 80
Lujan, Roy, 49
Lummis, Charles, 39, 41
Lumpkins, William, 97
Lux, Guillermo, 97

M
Mabel Dodge Luhan House, 76–77,
   79, 80, 112
Macaione, Tommy, 143, 144
Mack, John, 151–152
Maltin, Leonard, 132, 133, 134–135
Man from Laramie, 161-2
Mandelman, Beatrice, 114
Marion Center for Photographic Arts,
   39–40, 43–44, 46
Martinez, Antonio José, 40
Martinez, Maria, 97
Martinez, Paige, 51
Martinez, Sefarino, 19
Masterson, Bat, 85
Maxwell Land Grant, 85
Maxwell, Lucien, 85
McCartney, Paul, 27, 29
McCartys, NM, 120
McCleery, Sue, 79
McCullough, David J., 37
McDonald, William G., 49
McGovern, George, 76
McKircher, Sam, 36
McLerie, Jeanie, 31–33

Mexican Revolution, 23–26
Mingenbach, John, 80
Mining, 32, 85
Mirabal, Eva, 111–115
Momaday, N. Scott, 14–15
Monongye, Jesse, 88
Montezuma Castle, 138, 140–142
Montoya, Geronima, 91
Montoya, Joseph, 74
Morgan, Thomas, 63–64
Morley, Ada, 123
Movies in New Mexico, 75–76, 81–83,
    130–135, 141, 157–162
Moylan, Lloyd, 99–100
Munden, Marjorie, 86
Museum of Fine Arts, 40, 47
Music in New Mexico, 27–33, 97,
    126–129
Myers, Joan, 44
Myers, Lee, 34

N
Nagatani, Patrick, 43
Nailor, Gerald, 113
Namingha, Dan, 88
Naranjo Morse, Nora, 91
Narbona Pass, NM, 65
National American Woman Suffrage
    Association, 122
National New Deal Preservation As-
    sociation, 96, 99
National Trust for Historic Preserva-
    tion, 142
Native American arts, 87–94
Native American languages, 65
Native American rights, 19–21,
    62–66, 125
Navajo Community College, 65
Navajos, 33, 42, 62–66
New Deal, The, 42, 95–100
New Mexican, 35–36, 38, 70, 90, 124,
    139, 143–4, 153–156
New Mexico geology, 116–121

New Mexico movie locations, 75–76,
    81–83, 141
New Mexico politics, 19–20, 34–38,
    49, 68–74
Newhall, Beaumont, 39, 42, 43, 44
Newhall, Nancy, 41, 44
Nichols, John, 77, 79
Nixon, Richard, 20, 21
Noggle, Anne, 43
Norman Petty Studio, 28–29, 30
North Carolina State University, 58,
    60
North, Duncan, 157–160
Northrup, Steve, 44
Nuzum, Jerry, 73–74

O
Oakley, Annie, 85
O'Brien, Tony, 44
O'Keeffe, Georgia, 41, 53
Okuma, Jamie, 89
Oñate, Juan de, 106–110
Opera, 126–129
Orbison, Roy, 30
Ortiz, Cleofes, 32
Ortiz y Pino, Gerald, 77
O'Sullivan, Timothy H., 30, 41, 42
Otero-Warren, Adelina, 123–124

P
ParkeHarrison, Robert, 43
Parson, Elsie Clews, 41
Patrick Smith Park, 144
Peñasco, NM, 97
Pershing, John J., 24, 25
Personal names, 62–66
Petroglyph National Monument, 120
Petty, Norman, 27–31
Petty, Vi, 31
Phenix, NM, 34
Phillips, Bert, 112
Philmont Scout Ranch, 84
Photo-Eye Books and Prints, 43, 46
Photography, 39–47, 97

Pie Town, NM, 42, 97
Pit, The, 58–61
Place names, 65
Pop Chalee, 97, 113
Porter, Eliot, 42, 43, 46
Powwow Highway, 162
Price, John, 149
Primitive Mysteries, 54
Prohibition, 34–38
Protas, Ron, 57
Pueblo Indians, 143

Q
Questa, NM, 97

R
Radin, Paul, 132
Ramirez, José Fernando, 107
Ranching, 85
Rangell, Paul, 32
Ravel, Sam, 25
Red Dawn, 162
Reed, Rixon, 46
Religious Crimes Act, 19
Remington, Frederic, 85
Review Santa Fe, 43
Ribak, Louis, 114
Richards, Keith, 27
Richardson, Jerry, 101–105
Rio Puerco Volcanic Necks, 120
Roberts, Gary L., 68, 69
Rock and roll, 27–31
Rocks with Wings, 104
Rodriguez, Alfred, 108
Rodriguez, Elena, 78–79
Rolling Stones, The, 29
Romero, Diego, 88
Romero, Juan de Jesus, 21
Romero, Mateo, 88
Roosevelt, Theodore, 17, 18
Root, John, 140
Roses (music group), 30
Roswell, NM, 133, 148–152
Rubinstein, Meridel, 43, 44

Russek, Janet, 43–4, 46
Rynerson, William Logan, 68, 70–71

S
Sakiestewa, Ramona, 91
Salazar, Roman, 144–147
Salgado, Sebastião, 40
Sanchez, Joseph, 108
Sando, Joe, 116–117
Santa Clara Pueblo, 116, 117, 118–119
Santa Domingo Pueblo, 89–90
Santa Fe Center for the Visual Arts, 43
Santa Fe Indian Market, 87–94
Santa Fe Indian School, 113
Santa Fe New Mexican. see New Mexican
Santa Fe, NM, 68–71, 87–94, 126–129, 143–147, 153–156, 157–160
Santa Fe Opera, 126–129
Santa Fe Photographic Workshops, 40, 43, 44, 46
Santa Fe Railroad, 112
Santa Fe Ring, 71
Santa Fe Weekly Gazette, 70–71
Saunders, Daniel, 151
Scheinbaum and Russek Photography, 43, 44, 46
Scheinbaum, David, 42, 44, 46
Schneider, Steve, 133
Sedillo, Dan, 74
Seligman, Siegmund, 40
Serna, Frank, 145
Shiprock High School, 101–105
Shiprock, NM, 102–103
Shorty, Perry, 88
Shuster, Will S., 34, 97
Simmons, Marc, 73
Site Santa Fe, 40
Sitzberger, Ed, 86
Slocum, Herbert, 25
Slough, John Potts, 68–71
Smiley, Sheila, 102
Smith, Andrew, 43, 44, 46
Society for the Preservation of Taos, 78

Southwestern Association for Indian
　　Arts, 88
Spanish Market, 97
Sports, 58–61, 101–105, 136–140
St. James Hotel, 84–86
Stevens, Doris, 123
Stodelle, Ernestine, 54–55
Strand, Paul, 39, 41, 42, 46
Stravinsky, Igor, 126–129
Stravinsky, Vera, 128–129
Strieber, Ann, 151
Strieber, Whitley, 150
Strong, Craig, 57
Suffrage Movement in New Mexico,
　　122–125
Sullivan, Niki, 30
Swentzell, Roxanne, 91

T

Tafoya, Lu Ann, 93
Tafoya, Margaret, 93
Tank Girl, 162
Tao of Steve, 157–160
Taos art colony, 41
Taos Moderns, 114
Taos News, 75–76, 76
Taos, NM, 75–80, 112, 114
Taos Pueblo, 17–22, 111–112
Taos Society of Artists, 112
Teapot Dome scandal, 72
Tenorio, Robert, 89–90
Terrell, Steve, 72–75, 155–156
Thorpe, Jack, 33
Three Ravens Fine Art, 45
Throckmorton-McDowell, Sharla,
　　133
Thumb, Tom, 85
Thumbelina, 85
Tourism, 26, 87–88, 112, 137–8, 148,
　　148–152
Trampas, NM, 42, 97
Truchas, NM, 57
Turner, Louise, 36

U

Udall, Stewart, 19
UFO Encounter Festival, 148–152
UFOs, 133, 148–152
United World College, 140, 142
University of New Mexico, 40, 42–3
University Arena, 58–61
U.S. Government policies, 17–20,
　　63–66

V

Valles Caldera, 116–119, 120
Valles, Domingo, 73
Valley of Fires State Recreation Area,
　　121
Valvano, Jim, 58, 60–61
Van Dyke, Willard, 41
Velarde, Pablita, 91, 97, 99, 113
Vicenti, Cowboy, 62–63
Vigil, Lasaro, 145
Vigil, Lonnie, 87–88, 92–93
Villa, Pancho, 23–26
Villagrá, Gaspar Peréz de, 106–110
Volcanoes in New Mexico, 116–121
Voss, Jane, 33
Vroman, Adam Clark, 41, 42

W

Wallace, Lew, 85
Walpole, Alton, 160
Warm Day, Jonathan, 112–113,
　　114–115
Warren, Alvin, 118–119
Washington Pass, NM, 65
Webb, Todd, 43
Weston, Edward, 39, 41–42, 44
Whitegeese, Daryl, 93–4
Wills, Bob, 32–33
Wills, Johnny Lee, 32
Wilson, Woodrow, 23, 24, 25
Witkin, Joel-Peter, 43, 47
Wittick, Ben, 41
Wolfpack, North Carolina State, 58,
　　60

Woman's Christian Temperance
      Union, 34–35
Works Projects Administration
      (WPA), 42, 95–100
Wright, T.J., 86

Y
Yates, Steve, 43, 45, 46–47, 96–99
Yazzie, Larry, 94
Young, Louis, 153–156
Young, Neil, 76

Z
Zapata, Emiliano, 24
Zuni Bandera Volcanic Field, 20
Zuni Pueblo, 54, 108–109
Zuni Salt Lake Crater, 121

CPSIA information can be obtained at www.ICGtesting.com
Printed in the USA
LVOW040944040312

271485LV00005B/176/A